Decoding Tomorrow's Currency: An In-Depth Exploration of the Future of Cryptocurrency

Randy Woodrum

Published by Randy Woodrum, 2024.

While every precaution has been taken in the preparation of this book, the publisher assumes no responsibility for errors or omissions, or for damages resulting from the use of the information contained herein.

DECODING TOMORROW'S CURRENCY: AN IN-DEPTH EXPLORATION OF THE FUTURE OF CRYPTOCURRENCY

First edition. March 11, 2024.

ISBN: 979-8224560318

Written by Randy Woodrum.

Decoding Tomorrow's Currency: An In-Depth Exploration of the Future of Cryptocurrency

I. Understanding Crypto Currency

In the vast universe of technological evolution, few phenomena have captured the collective imagination and disrupted traditional paradigms as profoundly as cryptocurrency. Born out of the enigmatic realms of blockchain technology, cryptocurrencies have emerged as a transformative force, challenging conventional notions of finance, security, and the very nature of currency itself.

Welcome to "Decoding Tomorrow's Currency: An In-Depth Exploration of the Future of Cryptocurrency." In the pages that follow, we embark on a journey into the heart of a digital revolution that is reshaping the way we conceive, transact, and interact with value. As we explore the intricate web of technologies, philosophies, and innovations that underpin the world of cryptocurrency, we seek to understand its present while deciphering the codes that illuminate its future.

Cryptocurrency, with its decentralized architecture and cryptographic foundations, has already demonstrated its disruptive potential. From the pioneering days of Bitcoin, where a pseudonymous creator introduced a revolutionary vision of peer-to-peer electronic cash, to the advent of smart contracts and decentralized finance (DeFi), the landscape has evolved at a staggering pace. Our mission in this exploration is to document this evolution and unravel the layers of complexity, speculation, and promise that envelop the future of money.

As we embark on this intellectual odyssey, we will encounter the groundbreaking technologies shaping tomorrow's currency—blockchain iterations beyond imagination, smart contracts poised to redefine agreements, and the integration of artificial intelligence with the immutable ledger. We will navigate the rise of decentralized finance, witnessing the birth of financial ecosystems that operate without intermediaries, transcending borders and empowering individuals in unprecedented ways.

The tokenization of assets will invite us into a realm where real-world valuables find representation in the form of cryptographic tokens—revolutionizing ownership, trading, and investment. Central Bank Digital Currencies (CBDCs) will blur the lines between the traditional and the digital, as nations contemplate the issuance of sovereign currencies on blockchain networks. Through these discussions, we will confront questions of regulation, privacy, and the environmental impact of this technological revolution.

The future of cryptocurrency extends beyond the technological domain. It is a force shaping societies, challenging power structures, and opening new frontiers for financial inclusion. As we contemplate the social and environmental impact of this digital renaissance, we find ourselves at the intersection of innovation, ethics, and global responsibility. "Decoding Tomorrow's Currency" is more than a chronicle of technological advancements; it is a guide to understanding the principles and philosophies that propel cryptocurrency into an uncertain future. It is an invitation to the curious, the skeptical, and the visionary alike—a call to engage with a future that unfolds in the encrypted language of innovation.

In the chapters that ensue, we will navigate through the diversity of cryptographic security, explore the rise of decentralized applications, dissect the intricacies of token economies, and grapple with the ethical considerations that accompany this transformative journey. Join us as we decipher the digital codes that herald the dawn of a new era in finance—a future where the very concept of money is rewritten in the indelible ink of blockchain. Welcome to the exploration of tomorrow's currency, where each chapter unveils a layer of the cryptographic world that is shaping the destiny of economies yet to come.

Definition and Brief History of Cryptocurrency

In the dynamic realm of finance and technology, cryptocurrency stands as a revolutionary concept—a digital offspring of cryptography and decentralized network architecture that has fundamentally altered our understanding of money, transactions, and trust. At its core, cryptocurrency is a form of digital or virtual currency that employs cryptographic techniques to secure financial transactions and control the creation of new units. Unlike traditional currencies issued by central authorities, cryptocurrencies operate on decentralized networks, providing users with a level of autonomy and security previously unseen in the financial world.

Defining Cryptocurrency:

Cryptocurrency derives its name from the fusion of two essential components: "crypto," representing the use of cryptographic techniques, and "currency," signifying its role as a medium of exchange. The cornerstone of cryptocurrencies is blockchain technology—a distributed ledger that records and verifies transactions across a network of computers. This decentralized ledger ensures transparency, security, and immutability, eliminating the need for a central authority to oversee and authenticate transactions.

Cryptocurrencies leverage cryptographic keys for secure digital signatures, enabling users to control the ownership and transfer of their assets. Public and private keys, along with decentralized consensus mechanisms, contribute to the resilience of the cryptocurrency ecosystem against fraud, hacking, and centralized manipulation.

Bitcoin, introduced in 2009 by the pseudonymous Satoshi Nakamoto, marked the genesis of cryptocurrencies and blockchain technology. It was conceived as a peer-to-peer electronic cash system, aiming to facilitate direct transactions without the need for intermediaries like banks. Bitcoin's underlying technology, blockchain, consists of a chain of blocks, each containing a list of transactions. These blocks are linked through cryptographic hashes, creating an unchangeable and transparent record of all transactions.

Brief History Timeline of Cryptocurrency:

Pre-Bitcoin Era

- The conceptual groundwork for cryptocurrency can be traced back to the cypherpunk movement of the 1980s and 1990s. Cypherpunks, advocating for privacy and security in the digital age, explored cryptographic solutions for financial transactions.

Bitcoin Emerges (2009)

- The release of Bitcoin's whitepaper by Satoshi Nakamoto in 2008 laid the theoretical foundation for cryptocurrency. In 2009, the Bitcoin software was implemented, and the first block, known as the "genesis block," was mined.

Early Developments (2010-2013)

- Bitcoin gained traction in online communities and began to be used for various transactions. In 2010, a programmer named Laszlo Hanyecz famously made the first real-world purchase with Bitcoin—two pizzas for 10,000 BTC. This period also saw the emergence of alternative cryptocurrencies, often referred to as "altcoins."

Rise of Altcoins and Innovation (2013-2016)

- Litecoin, introduced by Charlie Lee, became one of the earliest successful altcoins, offering faster transaction confirmation times. Other innovative cryptocurrencies like Ripple and Namecoin explored different use cases, paving the way for diversity in the crypto space.

Ethereum and Smart Contracts (2015)

- Ethereum, proposed by Vitalik Buterin, brought a new dimension to the cryptocurrency landscape with the introduction of smart contracts. These self-executing contracts paved the way for decentralized applications (DApps) and expanded the possibilities beyond simple peer-to-peer transactions.

ICO Boom and Regulatory Scrutiny (2017-2018)

- The Initial Coin Offering (ICO) trend gained momentum, allowing blockchain projects to raise funds through the sale of their tokens. However, regulatory scrutiny increased as fraudulent activities surfaced, leading to a more cautious environment.

Decentralized Finance (DeFi) and Continued Innovation (2019-Present)

- The decentralized finance movement gained prominence,

introducing financial services like lending, borrowing, and trading without traditional intermediaries. Cryptocurrency continued to evolve, with ongoing developments in scalability, privacy, and interoperability.

Today, the cryptocurrency landscape is vast and diverse, encompassing thousands of cryptocurrencies with varying use cases and technologies. The journey from Bitcoin's inception to the present day reflects technological advancements with the resilience and adaptability of a financial paradigm that continues to challenge and reshape traditional notions of currency and finance. As we stand at the crossroads of technological innovation, the future of cryptocurrency promises continued evolution, presenting both opportunities and challenges on the horizon.

Significance and Impact on the Financial Landscape

The emergence of cryptocurrency has ushered in a seismic shift in the financial landscape, disrupting traditional models and challenging the fundamental structures that have governed global economies for centuries. The significance of cryptocurrency lies in its role as a novel form of digital currency and in its potential to redefine the very essence of money and financial transactions.

At its core, cryptocurrency introduces a decentralized paradigm, eliminating the need for traditional intermediaries such as banks and financial institutions. This decentralization is facilitated by blockchain technology, a distributed ledger that records and verifies transactions across a network of computers. The significance of this decentralized approach is profound, as it enhances transparency, reduces reliance on centralized authorities, and mitigates the risks associated with single points of failure.

The impact of cryptocurrency on the financial landscape is multifaceted, encompassing various dimensions that extend beyond mere transactions. One of the most notable aspects is financial inclusion. Cryptocurrencies provide access to financial services for individuals who are unbanked or underbanked, transcending geographical barriers and bringing millions into the global economy. This inclusivity has the potential to reshape economic structures, empowering individuals who were previously excluded from traditional banking systems.

Moreover, cryptocurrency challenges the conventional understanding of money as a sovereign-backed, physical entity. With digital currencies like Bitcoin and Ethereum gaining widespread acceptance, the notion of a stateless, borderless currency becomes a reality. This shift holds profound implications for cross-border transactions, offering a decentralized alternative to the traditional financial system that is often encumbered by bureaucratic processes and high fees.

The impact of cryptocurrency is perhaps most evident in the realm of remittances. Migrant workers, who contribute significantly to global economies, often face exorbitant fees and slow processing times when sending money across borders. Cryptocurrencies provide a more efficient and cost-effective alternative, enabling near-instantaneous transactions with lower fees, thereby revolutionizing the remittance landscape.

Furthermore, the advent of blockchain technology and smart contracts has opened the door to a new era of financial innovation. Smart contracts, self-executing agreements with the terms directly written into code, eliminate the need for intermediaries in contractual relationships. This streamlines processes and reduces the potential for disputes and fraud, laying the groundwork for a more transparent and efficient financial ecosystem.

While the impact of cryptocurrency is transformative, it is not without challenges. Regulatory uncertainties, security concerns, and the volatile nature of cryptocurrency prices pose hurdles to widespread adoption. Governments and regulatory bodies grapple with the task of developing frameworks that balance innovation with the need for consumer protection and financial stability.

The significance of cryptocurrency also extends to its role as a store of value and investment. Bitcoin, often referred to as "digital gold," has garnered attention as a hedge against inflation and economic uncertainties. Institutional adoption of cryptocurrencies as an asset class further underscores their growing importance within the broader financial landscape.

The significance and impact of cryptocurrency on the financial landscape are profound and far-reaching. From decentralized transactions and financial inclusion to the evolution of smart contracts and the emergence of new investment paradigms, cryptocurrency has become a catalyst for change. As we navigate this dynamic landscape, the transformative potential of cryptocurrency continues to unfold, challenging established norms and offering a glimpse into the future of finance—one where decentralized and borderless digital currencies play a central role in shaping the global economy.

The purpose and scope of "Decoding Tomorrow's Currency: An In-Depth Exploration of the Future of Cryptocurrency" extend far beyond a mere examination of digital currencies. This book aims to provide readers with a comprehensive and knowledgeable understanding of the multifaceted world of cryptocurrency, looking into its technological intricacies, historical evolution, and the profound impact it holds on to the future of finance.

At its core, this book seeks to demystify the complex landscape of cryptocurrency for a diverse audience. Whether you are a newcomer intrigued by the concept of digital currencies or a seasoned investor navigating the intricacies of blockchain technology, the book endeavors to be a guiding companion on your journey. The purpose is not to present cryptocurrency as a singular entity but to unravel the layers of innovation, challenges, and potential within this dynamic ecosystem.

The scope of the book spans the entire spectrum of cryptocurrency, encompassing foundational concepts, cutting-edge technologies, and the socio-economic implications of this financial revolution. From the rudimentary principles of blockchain and the inception of Bitcoin to the rise of decentralized finance (DeFi) and the tokenization of assets, each chapter meticulously explores a facet of this rapidly evolving landscape. By doing so, the book aspires to equip readers with the knowledge necessary to navigate the complexities of cryptocurrency confidently.

The book extends its scope to address the broader implications of cryptocurrency on society, governance, and the global economy. Cryptocurrency is not just a novel means of exchanging value; it represents a paradigm shift that challenges traditional power structures, questions established norms, and introduces unprecedented opportunities and risks. The exploration of these broader themes aims to spark critical thinking and encourage readers to contemplate the profound transformations underway in the financial world.

The purpose of "Decoding Tomorrow's Currency" is to provide speculative forecast and to foster an informed and intelligent dialogue around the future of cryptocurrency. In doing so, the book engages with key questions that extend beyond technology, touching upon ethical considerations, regulatory challenges, and the environmental impact of decentralized systems. By addressing these complex issues, the book invites readers to think critically about the responsible development and adoption of cryptocurrency in a rapidly changing world.

As the cryptocurrency landscape evolves, so too does the book's exploration. The scope includes insights from thought leaders, industry experts, and pioneers who have shaped the trajectory of this digital revolution. Interviews, case studies, and real-world examples enrich the narrative, offering a holistic perspective that captures the dynamic and sometimes unpredictable nature of the cryptocurrency ecosystem.

In essence, the purpose and scope of this book converge on the idea of empowerment through knowledge. Cryptocurrency represents more than just a technological advancement; it embodies a transformative force that has the potential to redefine the very nature of trust, value, and financial transactions. By embarking on this exploration, readers are invited to participate in the ongoing conversation about the future of money, to challenge assumptions, and to envision a financial landscape shaped by the principles of decentralization, transparency, and innovation. In the pages that follow, "Decoding Tomorrow's Currency" endeavors to serve as a comprehensive guide—a roadmap that empowers readers to navigate the complexities of cryptocurrency

with clarity, curiosity, and a deep appreciation for the transformative
potential that lies ahead.

II. The Evolution of Cryptocurrency

Overview of Early Cryptocurrencies (Bitcoin, Litecoin, etc.)

The emergence of early cryptocurrencies, spearheaded by the groundbreaking introduction of Bitcoin, laid the foundation for a transformative shift in the financial landscape. This chapter provides a comprehensive overview of the pioneering digital currencies that paved the way for the diverse ecosystem we witness today.

Bitcoin: The Genesis of Cryptocurrency

Bitcoin, introduced in 2009 by the mysterious figure or group known as Satoshi Nakamoto, stands as the inaugural and most iconic cryptocurrency. Conceived as a decentralized, peer-to-peer electronic cash system, Bitcoin aimed to enable secure and transparent transactions without the need for intermediaries. Its underlying technology, blockchain, served as a distributed ledger, recording every transaction across a network of computers in an immutable and transparent manner.

Bitcoin's significance extends beyond its role as a digital currency; it represents a philosophical departure from traditional financial systems. The issuance of Bitcoin is capped at 21 million, fostering a deflationary model that contrasts with fiat currencies subject to inflationary pressures. Bitcoin's decentralized nature, secured by a consensus mechanism called Proof of Work (PoW), empowers users with autonomy over their financial transactions and challenges the authority of centralized entities.

Litecoin: The Silver to Bitcoin's Gold

Following the success of Bitcoin, Litecoin emerged in 2011 as one of the earliest altcoins, often referred to as the "silver to Bitcoin's gold."

Created by Charlie Lee, a former Google engineer, Litecoin aimed to offer a faster and more scalable alternative to Bitcoin. Its architecture, based on a different hashing algorithm called Scrypt, enabled quicker block generation and enhanced transaction confirmation times.

Litecoin's introduction further diversified the cryptocurrency landscape, demonstrating that variations in technology and design could address specific shortcomings or limitations perceived in the original cryptocurrency. Litecoin's acceptance highlighted the potential for alternative digital currencies to coexist and cater to different use cases within the broader ecosystem.

Namecoin: Pioneering Decentralized Domain Registration

In the quest for extending blockchain technology beyond the realm of digital currency, Namecoin emerged in 2011 as a pioneering project. Functioning as both a cryptocurrency and a decentralized domain name system (DNS), Namecoin aimed to provide censorship-resistant domain registration. By leveraging blockchain for domain management, Namecoin sought to decentralize a crucial aspect of the internet infrastructure, laying the groundwork for future blockchain applications beyond financial transactions.

Peercoin: Introducing Proof of Stake

The introduction of Peercoin in 2012 brought forth a novel consensus mechanism—Proof of Stake (PoS). While Bitcoin and Litecoin relied on energy intensive PoW, Peercoin's PoS aimed to address environmental concerns and promote energy efficiency. PoS operates based on the ownership of cryptocurrency rather than computational power, reducing the ecological impact associated with traditional mining.

The overview of these early cryptocurrencies underscores the diversity of thought and experimentation within the nascent cryptocurrency space. Bitcoin's establishment as a decentralized currency set the stage for innovative variations and expansions of the blockchain concept. Litecoin, Namecoin, and Peercoin, among others, introduced alternative features and consensus mechanisms, contributing to the evolving narrative of decentralized technologies.

As we explore the formative years of cryptocurrencies, it becomes evident that the early experiments laid the groundwork for the vibrant and complex ecosystem witnessed today. The innovations, challenges, and lessons from these early pioneers have shaped the trajectory of digital currencies, setting the stage for ongoing exploration and advancements in the decentralized financial frontier.

Technological Advancements (Blockchain, Smart Contracts, etc.)

The evolution of cryptocurrencies goes hand in hand with a series of technological advancements that have defined their capabilities and expanded the horizon of possibilities for the broader blockchain ecosystem. At the heart of this technological revolution lies blockchain, the foundational innovation that underpins most cryptocurrencies. Blockchain is a distributed ledger that records transactions across a network of computers, ensuring transparency, security, and immutability.

The technological advancements in cryptocurrency and blockchain space have expanded the capabilities of digital currencies while paving the way for a decentralized future. From the foundational innovation of blockchain to the sophisticated smart contracts, decentralized finance, and emerging consensus mechanisms, each advancement contributes to the ongoing narrative of a transformative force that is reshaping the financial landscape and beyond. As these technologies continue to mature, their impact is likely to extend into realms yet unexplored, further defining the contours of the decentralized era.

Blockchain Technology

Blockchain, often described as a decentralized and distributed ledger, forms the backbone of most cryptocurrencies. It operates on a consensus mechanism, where transactions are validated by a network of nodes through cryptographic algorithms. Each block in the chain contains a cryptographic hash of the previous block, creating a linked and tamper-resistant chain. The decentralized nature of blockchain eliminates the need for intermediaries, providing a transparent and secure framework for peer-to-peer transactions.

Smart Contracts

A significant leap beyond the simple transfer of digital currencies, smart contracts emerged as a transformative technological advancement, pioneered by the Ethereum blockchain. Smart contracts are self-executing contracts with the terms directly written into code. They automatically execute predefined actions when specific conditions are met, eliminating the need for intermediaries, and enhancing the efficiency and transparency of contractual agreements. Smart contracts have extended the use of blockchain beyond mere transactions, enabling the creation of decentralized applications (DApps) and fostering the growth of decentralized finance (DeFi) platforms.

Decentralized Finance (DeFi)

The advent of blockchain and smart contracts has given rise to the decentralized finance movement. DeFi represents a paradigm shift in traditional financial systems, offering decentralized alternatives to various financial services such as lending, borrowing, and trading. DeFi platforms, built on blockchain networks, operate without the need for traditional intermediaries like banks. This democratization of finance opens new avenues for global financial inclusion, as users worldwide can access these services with nothing more than an internet connection.

Interoperability and Cross-Chain Solutions

As the blockchain landscape has expanded, interoperability has become a crucial focus for the industry. Interoperability allows different blockchains to communicate and share information seamlessly. Various projects and protocols have emerged to address this challenge, aiming to create a connected and interoperable blockchain ecosystem. Cross-chain solutions facilitate communication and value transfer between different blockchain networks, fostering collaboration and expanding the scope of blockchain applications.

Consensus Mechanisms

In the quest for scalability, energy efficiency, and consensus diversity, alternative consensus mechanisms have emerged. While Proof of Work (PoW) remains the original and widely adopted consensus mechanism, alternatives like Proof of Stake (PoS), Delegated Proof of Stake (DPoS), and others have gained prominence. These mechanisms offer different approaches to validating transactions and securing the network, each with its unique set of advantages and challenges.

Privacy and Security Solutions

The emphasis on privacy within blockchain networks has led to the development of privacy-focused cryptocurrencies and protocols. Cryptocurrencies like Monero and Zcash use advanced cryptographic techniques to obfuscate transaction details, providing enhanced privacy for users. Security solutions, including advanced encryption methods and secure multi-party computation, contribute to the ongoing efforts to fortify blockchain networks against potential threats and attacks.

Scalability Solutions

Addressing scalability challenges has been a critical aspect of technological advancements in the blockchain space. Layer 2 solutions, such as the Lightning Network for Bitcoin and state channels for Ethereum, aim to increase transaction throughput and reduce congestion on the main blockchain. These off-chain scaling solutions complement on-chain improvements and contribute to the overall scalability of blockchain networks.

Emergence of Altcoins and Tokenization

The cryptocurrency landscape, initially dominated by Bitcoin, experienced a significant expansion with the emergence of alternative cryptocurrencies, commonly referred to as altcoins. While Bitcoin pioneered the concept of digital currency and decentralized transactions, altcoins introduced variations in technology, governance, and use cases, contributing to the diversification of the crypto ecosystem.

The emergence of altcoins and the concept of tokenization have profoundly shaped the cryptocurrency landscape, providing alternatives to Bitcoin, and unlocking new possibilities beyond digital currencies. The evolution from simple alternatives to exploring diverse use cases, including decentralized finance and tokenized assets, reflects the dynamic nature of the blockchain industry. As the ecosystem continues to mature, altcoins and tokenization are likely to play pivotal roles in defining the future of finance and digital ownership.

The Pioneering Era of Altcoins

As Bitcoin gained traction in the early years, developers and innovators sought to explore alternative approaches to digital currencies. This led to the creation of numerous altcoins, each with its unique features and value propositions. Litecoin, introduced by Charlie Lee in 2011, was one of the first altcoins and aimed to provide a faster transaction confirmation time compared to Bitcoin. Litecoin's success demonstrated that variations in technology could address specific concerns and offer alternatives within the cryptocurrency space.

Diversification of Use Cases

Beyond serving as alternatives to Bitcoin, altcoins began to explore diverse use cases. Ripple (XRP), for instance, focused on facilitating fast and low-cost international money transfers, aiming to disrupt the traditional banking system. Ethereum, introduced by Vitalik Buterin in 2015, marked a paradigm shift by introducing a platform for decentralized applications (DApps) and smart contracts. This innovation opened the door to a wide array of use cases, including decentralized finance (DeFi), non-fungible tokens (NFTs), and more.

Tokenization: The Evolution of Digital Assets

Tokenization emerged as a pivotal concept, representing the conversion of real-world assets into digital tokens on a blockchain. This process expanded the scope of blockchain technology beyond currency, allowing for the representation of ownership or rights to various assets. Real estate, art, stocks, and even intellectual property could now be represented as tokens on a blockchain. This trend significantly increased the liquidity and accessibility of traditionally illiquid assets, unlocking new opportunities for investors and reducing barriers to entry for a broader range of participants.

ICO Boom and the Rise of Utility Tokens

The Initial Coin Offering (ICO) boom around 2017 marked a notable chapter in the evolution of altcoins and tokenization. ICOs provided a fundraising mechanism where projects could issue their tokens to the public in exchange for capital. These tokens, often referred to as utility tokens, represented access to a particular product or service within the issuing project's ecosystem. While ICOs facilitated rapid fundraising, they also faced criticisms for potential fraud and lack of regulatory oversight.

Security Tokens and Regulatory Compliance

The ICO boom prompted increased scrutiny from regulatory authorities, leading to a shift in the landscape toward more regulated and compliant offerings. Security tokens emerged as a response, representing digital assets subject to securities regulations. Security tokens differ from utility tokens in that they often represent ownership in a real-world asset and must comply with relevant securities laws. This shift toward compliance signaled a maturation of the tokenization space, aligning it more closely with existing regulatory frameworks.

Decentralized Finance (DeFi) and the Token Economy

The concept of decentralized finance (DeFi) gained prominence, leveraging tokenization to recreate traditional financial services on blockchain networks. DeFi protocols offered lending, borrowing, trading, and yield farming without the need for traditional intermediaries. The decentralized nature of these platforms, often governed by community-driven protocols, marked a significant departure from centralized finance systems.

Challenges and Opportunities

While the emergence of altcoins and tokenization brought forth innovation and new opportunities, it also presented challenges. The sheer diversity of projects, coupled with varying degrees of regulatory clarity, led to instances of fraud and scams within the space. Regulatory bodies globally have grappled with defining and overseeing the rapidly evolving landscape.

Regulatory Developments and Challenges

The rapid growth and global adoption of cryptocurrencies have prompted regulatory authorities worldwide to grapple with the challenge of creating a legal framework that balances innovation with consumer protection, financial stability, and the prevention of illicit activities. Regulatory developments in the cryptocurrency space have evolved significantly, reflecting an ongoing effort to understand and adapt to the dynamic nature of this emerging technology.

The cryptocurrency regulatory landscape is expected to undergo further refinement and adaptation. Regulatory authorities are likely to explore frameworks that address existing challenges and anticipate future developments in technology and market dynamics. Collaboration between the public and private sectors, along with ongoing engagement with the cryptocurrency community, will play a crucial role in shaping a regulatory environment that encourages responsible innovation and protects the interests of all stakeholders.

Early Regulatory Landscape

In the early years of cryptocurrencies, regulatory responses varied widely across jurisdictions. Some countries embraced digital currencies as a technological innovation, while others were cautious, citing concerns related to money laundering, fraud, and the potential use of cryptocurrencies for illegal activities. The decentralized and borderless nature of cryptocurrencies presented a unique challenge for regulators accustomed to traditional financial systems.

Recognition and Integration

As the cryptocurrency market matured, several countries recognized the potential benefits of blockchain technology and digital currencies. Regulatory frameworks began to take shape to provide clarity on how these assets would be treated. Some jurisdictions introduced licensing regimes for cryptocurrency exchanges, while others classified digital assets under existing securities or commodities laws. The recognition of cryptocurrency as a legitimate asset class marked a pivotal shift, with governments acknowledging the need for regulation to foster responsible innovation.

Anti-Money Laundering (AML) and Know Your Customer (KYC) Compliance

One of the primary regulatory focuses has been on combating money laundering and ensuring the integrity of the financial system. Many jurisdictions implemented stringent AML and KYC regulations for cryptocurrency exchanges and service providers, requiring them to verify the identity of users and report suspicious activities. These measures aimed to align the cryptocurrency space with established financial industry standards and enhance the accountability of market participants.

Security and Investor Protection

In response to the proliferation of initial coin offerings (ICOs) and token sales, regulators turned their attention to investor protection. Several jurisdictions issued warnings and guidelines to inform the public about the risks associated with investing in cryptocurrency projects. Some introduced requirements for companies conducting token offerings to register as securities or adhere to specific disclosure standards. The objective was to safeguard investors from fraudulent schemes and ensure transparency in fundraising activities.

Taxation and Reporting Requirements

The taxation of cryptocurrency transactions became another critical aspect of regulatory consideration. Different jurisdictions adopted diverse approaches, classifying cryptocurrencies as commodities, currencies, or assets subject to capital gains tax. Tax reporting requirements for cryptocurrency transactions were introduced to prevent tax evasion and ensure that individuals and businesses accurately reported their cryptocurrency-related income.

Stablecoins and Central Bank Digital Currencies (CBDCs)

The rise of stablecoins, pegged to fiat currencies or other assets, posed new challenges for regulators. Concerns about potential risks to financial stability and the need to safeguard consumers prompted regulatory scrutiny. Some jurisdictions issued guidelines for the issuance and operation of stablecoins, emphasizing the importance of transparency and reserve adequacy.

Central Bank Digital Currencies (CBDCs) also entered the regulatory discourse, with several central banks exploring the development of digital versions of their national currencies. The potential impact of CBDCs on monetary policy, financial stability, and the broader economy prompted regulators to assess and adapt their regulatory frameworks accordingly.

Global Cooperation and Standards

The decentralized nature of cryptocurrencies and their global reach necessitated increased international cooperation among regulators. Organizations like the Financial Action Task Force (FATF) set global standards for AML and KYC compliance in the cryptocurrency sector. The sharing of information and best practices became essential as regulators sought to address cross-border challenges and maintain the integrity of the global financial system.

Challenges and Future Considerations

Despite progress in regulatory developments, challenges persist. The evolving nature of the cryptocurrency space, rapid technological advancements, and the borderless nature of blockchain networks continue to test the effectiveness of regulatory frameworks. Striking the right balance between fostering innovation and mitigating risks remains an ongoing challenge.

23

III. Key Technologies Shaping the Future

Blockchain 3.0 and Beyond

As the cryptocurrency landscape continues to evolve, the concept of Blockchain 3.0 has emerged, representing the next phase of development beyond the foundational technologies introduced by Bitcoin and Ethereum. Blockchain 3.0 envisions a more scalable, interoperable, and user-friendly ecosystem, addressing limitations observed in earlier iterations.

Blockchain 3.0 represents a maturation and refinement of blockchain technology, incorporating lessons learned from earlier iterations and addressing their limitations. The ongoing exploration of scalability solutions, interoperability, enhanced privacy and security measures, advanced smart contracts, tokenization of real-world assets, sustainability efforts, and innovative governance models collectively shape the trajectory of blockchain technology beyond its foundational stages. As the ecosystem continues to evolve, Blockchain 3.0 sets the stage for a more inclusive, interconnected, and user-friendly blockchain future.

Scalability Solutions

One of the primary challenges faced by early blockchain networks, notably Bitcoin and Ethereum, is scalability. As these networks grew in popularity, concerns arose about their ability to handle a large number of transactions efficiently. Blockchain 3.0 seeks to address this issue through the implementation of various scalability solutions. Layer 2 scaling solutions, such as the Lightning Network for Bitcoin and state channels for Ethereum, aim to process transactions off-chain, reducing congestion on the main blockchain and increasing transaction throughput. Additionally, novel consensus mechanisms and sharding techniques are being explored to further enhance scalability.

Interoperability

Blockchain 3.0 places a strong emphasis on interoperability, enabling different blockchain networks to seamlessly communicate and share information. The lack of interoperability has been a hindrance to the widespread adoption of blockchain technology, as separate networks often operate in isolation. Projects and protocols are now actively working on creating standards and protocols that facilitate interoperability, allowing for the free flow of data and value between different blockchains. This interoperability is essential for creating a more connected and collaborative blockchain ecosystem.

Cross-Chain Solutions

Building on the idea of interoperability, cross-chain solutions have gained prominence in Blockchain 3.0. These solutions facilitate communication and value transfer between different blockchain networks, allowing users to interact with assets and smart contracts across multiple chains. Cross-chain platforms aim to overcome the limitations of siloed blockchains, offering a more cohesive and interconnected experience for users and developers alike.

Enhanced Privacy and Security Measures

Blockchain 3.0 places a heightened focus on privacy and security, recognizing the importance of protecting user data and transactions. Privacy-focused cryptocurrencies, utilizing advanced cryptographic techniques such as zero-knowledge proofs, aim to provide enhanced anonymity for users. Security measures are also evolving, with advanced encryption methods and secure multi-party computation being explored to fortify blockchain networks against potential threats and attacks. These enhancements contribute to the creation of a more robust and secure environment for blockchain users.

Smart Contracts and Decentralized Applications (DApps)

While smart contracts and decentralized applications (DApps) were pivotal in Blockchain 2.0 (Ethereum's era), Blockchain 3.0 aims to refine and expand these capabilities. Smart contracts, self-executing agreements with the terms directly written into code, are becoming more sophisticated and versatile. They play a crucial role in automating a wide range of processes beyond simple financial transactions. Decentralized applications are evolving to offer user-friendly interfaces and seamless experiences, making blockchain technology more accessible to a broader audience.

Tokenization of Real-World Assets

Blockchain 3.0 explores the tokenization of real-world assets, expanding beyond the representation of digital currencies. This involves converting tangible and intangible assets, such as real estate, art, stocks, and intellectual property, into digital tokens on a blockchain. Tokenization provides increased liquidity, fractional ownership opportunities, and simplified transfer of ownership for traditionally illiquid assets. This innovation opens up new possibilities for investors and contributes to the democratization of financial markets.

Sustainability and Green Blockchain

Amid growing concerns about the environmental impact of blockchain networks that use energy-intensive consensus mechanisms like Proof of Work (PoW), Blockchain 3.0 seeks to embrace more sustainable alternatives. Transitioning towards consensus mechanisms that are environmentally friendly, such as Proof of Stake (PoS) and delegated consensus, aligns with the broader goals of achieving sustainability in blockchain operations.

Governance Models

Blockchain 3.0 is exploring novel governance models that aim to achieve a more decentralized decision-making process. These models go beyond the traditional mechanisms seen in earlier blockchain iterations and involve a more inclusive and community-driven approach to network governance. This evolution is crucial for ensuring that blockchain networks remain adaptable and responsive to the needs of their user communities.

Interoperability Solutions

Interoperability has emerged as a critical challenge in the blockchain space, as the proliferation of diverse blockchain networks has highlighted the need for seamless communication and collaboration between these decentralized systems. Interoperability solutions in the blockchain ecosystem aim to create a more interconnected and cohesive environment, enabling the free flow of information, value, and assets across different blockchain platforms.

Interoperability solutions play a pivotal role in shaping the future of blockchain technology. As the ecosystem continues to mature, these solutions contribute to a more connected and collaborative blockchain environment. The development of interoperability standards, cross-chain communication protocols, and innovative projects like Cosmos and Polkadot mark significant steps toward realizing the vision of a seamlessly interconnected blockchain ecosystem. Looking ahead, the ongoing evolution of interoperability solutions is likely to play a central role in fostering a more inclusive and efficient blockchain landscape.

The Challenge of Siloed Blockchains

The early years of blockchain development saw the creation of various networks with unique features, consensus mechanisms, and use cases. While this diversity fueled innovation, it also resulted in siloed blockchains that operated independently of one another. This lack of interoperability hindered the full potential of blockchain technology, preventing efficient communication and collaboration between different networks.

Cross-Chain Communication Protocols

To address the challenge of interoperability, developers and projects have introduced cross-chain communication protocols. These protocols establish standards for how different blockchains can communicate and share information. Examples include the Interledger Protocol (ILP), Polkadot, and Cosmos. These protocols enable the transfer of assets and data between disparate blockchain networks, fostering a more interconnected ecosystem.

Cosmos: Building an Internet of Blockchains

Cosmos, a prominent project in the interoperability space, introduces the concept of an "Internet of Blockchains." Cosmos aims to create a network of interconnected blockchains, known as zones, that can communicate and transact with each other. The Cosmos Hub serves as the central hub connecting these zones. This architecture allows for the transfer of assets and data between different blockchains within the Cosmos ecosystem.

Polkadot: A Multichain Network for Interoperability

Polkadot is another significant player in the interoperability landscape. Founded by Dr. Gavin Wood, one of Ethereum's co-founders, Polkadot introduces a relay chain that connects multiple blockchains, referred to as parachains. These parachains can have their unique characteristics while benefiting from shared security and interoperability facilitated by the relay chain. Polkadot's design allows for scalability and flexibility in the creation and interaction of diverse blockchains.

Atomic Swaps and Decentralized Exchanges

Atomic swaps represent a decentralized mechanism for exchanging assets across different blockchains without the need for intermediaries. This technology allows users to swap one cryptocurrency directly for another, even if they exist on separate blockchain networks. Decentralized exchanges (DEXs) leverage atomic swap technology to enable peer-to-peer trading of assets across various blockchains, promoting a more fluid and interconnected market.

Wrapped Tokens and Cross-Chain Bridges

Wrapped tokens are a form of representing assets from one blockchain on another. These tokens are pegged to the value of the underlying asset and can be moved across different blockchains. Cross-chain bridges facilitate the transfer of these wrapped tokens between blockchains, enabling users to interact with assets from different networks seamlessly. Ethereum's Wrapped Bitcoin (WBTC) is a notable example, representing Bitcoin on the Ethereum blockchain.

Interledger Protocol (ILP)

The Interledger Protocol is designed to facilitate payments between different payment networks. ILP acts as a protocol for connecting ledgers, whether they are blockchain-based or traditional financial ledgers. It enables the routing of payments across different networks, allowing for interoperability between diverse financial systems. ILP has been embraced for its potential to bridge the gap between various payment networks, including both traditional and blockchain-based systems.

Challenges and Future Considerations

Despite the progress in interoperability solutions, challenges remain. Standardizing communication protocols, ensuring security in cross-chain transactions, and achieving consensus on interoperability standards across the industry are ongoing considerations. Additionally, regulatory frameworks must adapt to the interconnected nature of blockchain networks.

Quantum Resistance

Quantum resistance has emerged as a critical consideration in the world of cryptography and blockchain technology, driven by the potential threat posed by quantum computers to traditional cryptographic algorithms. As quantum computing technology advances, there is growing concern that these powerful machines could break widely used encryption methods, rendering current security protocols obsolete. Quantum resistance, also known as post-quantum cryptography, involves developing cryptographic algorithms that can withstand the computational capabilities of quantum computers, ensuring the continued security and integrity of digital systems.

Quantum Computers and Cryptographic Vulnerabilities

Traditional cryptographic methods, such as those based on factoring large numbers or solving discrete logarithm problems, form the foundation of secure communication and data protection in the digital realm. However, quantum computers have the potential to solve these problems exponentially faster than classical computers through algorithms like Shor's algorithm. This capacity poses a significant threat to the security of widely used encryption schemes, including RSA and ECC (Elliptic Curve Cryptography), which underpin much of today's digital infrastructure.

Post-Quantum Cryptography

Post-quantum cryptography involves the development and adoption of cryptographic algorithms that are resistant to attacks by quantum computers. These algorithms aim to provide a level of security that withstands the power of quantum computation, ensuring the confidentiality and integrity of sensitive information. Research in post-quantum cryptography spans various mathematical approaches, such as lattice-based cryptography, hash-based cryptography, code-based cryptography, and multivariate polynomial cryptography, among others.

Lattice-Based Cryptography

Lattice-based cryptography is considered one of the leading candidates for post-quantum security. It relies on the mathematical properties of lattices, which are complex geometric structures. The hardness of certain lattice problems forms the basis for cryptographic functions. Lattice-based cryptography offers a high degree of security and is resistant to attacks by both classical and quantum computers. This approach is being explored for applications like digital signatures, key exchange, and encryption.

Hash-Based Cryptography

Hash-based cryptography leverages the properties of cryptographic hash functions for secure communication. While quantum computers can perform operations exponentially faster, hash-based algorithms, such as the Merkle tree-based Lamport signature, remain secure even against quantum adversaries. These algorithms provide a foundation for creating digital signatures and ensuring data integrity in a post-quantum era.

Code-Based Cryptography

Code-based cryptography relies on the complexity of error-correcting codes to resist attacks by quantum computers. The McEliece cryptosystem is an example of a code-based cryptographic scheme. It is based on the difficulty of decoding random linear codes, making it a promising candidate for secure communication in the quantum computing age. The robustness of code-based cryptography stems from the difficulty of solving certain mathematical problems associated with linear codes.

Challenges and Adoption

While post-quantum cryptographic algorithms offer promising solutions, their adoption faces challenges. Transitioning from widely established cryptographic standards to new, quantum-resistant algorithms requires careful consideration of compatibility, implementation, and interoperability. The cryptographic community and standardization bodies are actively working to define and standardize post-quantum cryptographic algorithms to ensure a smooth transition and maintain the security of digital systems.

Blockchain and Quantum Resistance

Blockchain technology relies heavily on cryptographic algorithms for securing transactions, digital signatures, and consensus mechanisms. The quantum threat prompts the blockchain community to explore and implement quantum-resistant cryptographic solutions. Cryptocurrencies like Bitcoin, which use SHA-256 for hashing and ECDSA for digital signatures, are vulnerable to quantum attacks. As a result, quantum-resistant alternatives are being explored for potential integration into blockchain protocols to safeguard against quantum threats.

Looking Ahead

The timeline for widespread adoption of quantum computers capable of breaking current cryptographic standards remains uncertain. However, the proactive development and implementation of quantum-resistant cryptographic algorithms represent a crucial step in ensuring the long-term security of digital systems. The intersection of quantum computing and cryptography is a dynamic and evolving space, with researchers, cryptographers, and technologists collaborating to stay ahead of potential quantum threats and secure the future of digital communication and information protection. As quantum computing technology progresses, the quantum resistance efforts will play a vital role in fortifying the foundations of cybersecurity.

Integration of Artificial Intelligence in Cryptocurrency

The integration of artificial intelligence (AI) in the realm of cryptocurrency represents a groundbreaking convergence of two transformative technologies, promising to reshape the landscape of digital finance and trading. AI, with its ability to analyze vast datasets, recognize patterns, and make informed predictions, brings a new dimension to the world of cryptocurrencies, enhancing efficiency, security, and decision-making processes across various aspects of the ecosystem.

The integration of artificial intelligence in cryptocurrency is a dynamic and transformative process that extends across various facets of the digital finance landscape. From automated trading and predictive analytics to enhanced security measures and decentralized financial services, AI-driven solutions are redefining how participants interact with and navigate the cryptocurrency ecosystem. As the synergy between AI and cryptocurrency continues to evolve, it holds the potential to unlock new levels of efficiency, accessibility, and innovation in the decentralized financial frontier.

Automated Trading Algorithms

One of the most visible integrations of AI in cryptocurrency is within automated trading algorithms. AI-driven trading bots leverage machine learning algorithms to analyze market data, historical trends, and real-time news feeds to execute trades on behalf of users. These algorithms can adapt to changing market conditions, identify trading opportunities, and execute orders at speeds far beyond human capabilities. Traders can use these bots to implement complex trading strategies, manage risk, and capitalize on market fluctuations with a level of precision and speed that was previously unattainable.

Predictive Analytics and Price Forecasting

AI's ability to analyze vast datasets enables the development of predictive analytics tools for price forecasting in the cryptocurrency market. Machine learning models can process historical price data, market sentiment, and various other factors to generate forecasts about future price movements. While cryptocurrency markets are known for their volatility, AI-powered analytics aim to provide traders and investors with valuable insights to make informed decisions, manage risks, and optimize their investment strategies.

Enhanced Security and Fraud Detection

AI plays a crucial role in bolstering security measures within the cryptocurrency space. Advanced AI algorithms are employed to detect and prevent fraudulent activities, including unauthorized access, phishing attacks, and fraudulent transactions. Machine learning models can learn from patterns of legitimate user behavior and quickly identify anomalies that may indicate malicious activities. This proactive approach to security is essential in an environment where the decentralized and pseudonymous nature of cryptocurrencies can attract various forms of cyber threats.

Personalized User Experiences

AI-driven personalization is becoming increasingly prevalent in cryptocurrency platforms. Exchanges and wallets leverage AI algorithms to analyze user behavior, preferences, and transaction history to deliver personalized experiences. This may include tailored investment suggestions, user interface customization, or personalized notifications based on individual trading patterns. The goal is to enhance user engagement and satisfaction by providing a more intuitive and relevant experience tailored to each user's needs.

Decentralized Finance (DeFi) and Smart Contracts

The integration of AI in decentralized finance (DeFi) platforms holds the potential to revolutionize the way financial services are delivered. AI-powered smart contracts can automate complex financial processes, such as lending, borrowing, and yield farming, without the need for traditional intermediaries. These smart contracts, driven by AI algorithms, can assess risk, determine interest rates, and execute transactions autonomously, contributing to the efficiency and accessibility of decentralized financial services.

Tokenomics and Tokenization

AI plays a role in shaping the tokenomics of cryptocurrencies and the broader concept of tokenization. Tokenomics refers to the economic model and incentives behind a cryptocurrency. AI can be utilized to optimize token distribution, governance mechanisms, and incentive structures within blockchain networks. Additionally, AI contributes to the tokenization of real-world assets, enabling the representation of physical assets like real estate, art, or commodities as digital tokens on blockchain networks. This intersection of AI and tokenization opens new possibilities for creating dynamic and intelligent economic systems.

Challenges and Ethical Considerations

While the integration of AI in cryptocurrency brings about numerous benefits, it also raises challenges and ethical considerations. The use of AI in trading, for instance, may lead to concerns about market manipulation and the exacerbation of market volatility. Additionally, issues related to privacy, data security, and the potential for biased algorithms are critical considerations that must be addressed to ensure the responsible and ethical use of AI in the cryptocurrency space.

IV. The Rise of Decentralized Finance (DeFi)

Understanding Decentralized Exchanges

Decentralized exchanges (DEXs) represent a pivotal evolution in the world of cryptocurrency trading, providing users with a decentralized and trustless platform for exchanging digital assets. Unlike traditional centralized exchanges that rely on intermediaries to facilitate trades and custody user funds, DEXs operate on blockchain technology, allowing users to retain control of their private keys and maintain ownership of their assets throughout the trading process. Understanding the key features, benefits, and challenges of decentralized exchanges is crucial for navigating the decentralized financial landscape.

Decentralized exchanges represent a significant advancement in the cryptocurrency ecosystem, offering users increased security, control, and privacy in their trading activities. As the technology continues to evolve and address challenges related to liquidity and user experience, DEXs are poised to play a central role in shaping the future of decentralized finance (DeFi) and providing a trustless environment for the global exchange of digital assets. Understanding the principles and functionalities of decentralized exchanges is essential for users seeking to navigate the decentralized financial landscape and harness the benefits of non-custodial trading.

Key Features of Decentralized Exchanges

Non-Custodial Trading

One of the fundamental features of DEXs is non-custodial trading. Users retain control of their private keys and funds, eliminating the need to deposit assets into a centralized exchange wallet. This significantly reduces the risk of hacking and unauthorized access associated with centralized custody.

Smart Contracts

DEXs leverage smart contracts to automate and execute trading functions. These self-executing contracts facilitate the peer-to-peer exchange of assets directly on the blockchain. Smart contracts govern various aspects of trading, including order matching, settlement, and asset custody.

Global Accessibility

Decentralized exchanges operate on blockchain networks, enabling users from around the world to access and trade digital assets without the need for geographical restrictions or reliance on a central authority. This global accessibility aligns with the decentralized ethos of cryptocurrencies.

Token Pairings and Liquidity Pools

DEXs allow users to trade various token pairings directly. Liquidity is provided by users who contribute their assets to liquidity pools, enabling the exchange to facilitate trades seamlessly. Users can participate in liquidity provision and earn fees for their contributions.

Privacy and Anonymity

In many DEXs, users can trade without the need for extensive identity verification. This enhances privacy and anonymity, aligning with the principles of decentralization and user empowerment.

Benefits of Decentralized Exchanges

Security: The non-custodial nature of DEXs enhances security by eliminating the central point of failure associated with centralized exchanges. Users have full control of their private keys, reducing the risk of hacking incidents and unauthorized access.

User Control and Ownership

DEXs empower users by allowing them to retain control and ownership of their assets. Users do not need to trust a third party with their funds, as smart contracts automate the trading process without the need for intermediaries.

Reduced Counterparty Risk

Traditional exchanges introduce counterparty risk, as users rely on the exchange to execute and settle trades. DEXs, facilitated by smart contracts, mitigate counterparty risk by automating the execution of trades and settlement directly on the blockchain.

Global Accessibility and Inclusivity

Decentralized exchanges provide access to a global user base, fostering inclusivity in the cryptocurrency market. Users from regions with limited access to traditional financial services can participate in decentralized trading without facing geographical restrictions.

Privacy and Anonymity

Users on DEXs often have the option to trade without extensive identity verification, offering enhanced privacy and anonymity. This feature aligns with the decentralized ethos of cryptocurrencies, providing users with greater control over their personal information.

Challenges and Considerations

Liquidity Concerns

Some DEXs face challenges related to liquidity, as the decentralized nature of these platforms relies on user-contributed liquidity pools. Less liquid markets may result in slippage and challenges executing large trades.

User Experience

While strides have been made to improve the user experience of DEXs, they may still be perceived as less user-friendly than centralized counterparts. Efforts are ongoing to enhance interfaces and make decentralized trading more accessible to a broader audience.

Regulatory Uncertainty

The regulatory landscape for decentralized exchanges is evolving, and regulatory uncertainty remains a challenge. Some DEXs aim to comply with existing regulations, while others operate with a more decentralized and permissionless approach, which may attract regulatory scrutiny.

Smart Contract Risks

The reliance on smart contracts introduces the risk of vulnerabilities and exploits. While advancements in smart contract security are ongoing, users must be cautious and conduct due diligence when interacting with DEXs to mitigate potential risks.

Smart Contracts in DeFi

Smart contracts are the backbone of decentralized finance (DeFi), revolutionizing traditional financial processes by automating and self-executing complex agreements without the need for intermediaries. Built on blockchain technology, smart contracts are programmable contracts with predefined rules and conditions that automatically execute when those conditions are met. In the context of DeFi, smart contracts play a transformative role, providing transparency, security, and efficiency in various financial applications.

Decentralized lending and borrowing have introduced a paradigm shift in the way individuals' access and provide liquidity within the financial system. The decentralized nature of these protocols aligns with the principles of blockchain technology, offering users greater financial inclusivity and control over their assets. As web space continues to evolve, addressing challenges and enhancing security measures will be crucial for the sustained growth and adoption of decentralized lending and borrowing in the global financial landscape.

Decentralized Financial Ecosystem

Smart contracts serve as the building blocks of DeFi applications, enabling the creation of decentralized financial services that operate on blockchain networks. These services encompass a wide range of functionalities, including lending, borrowing, decentralized exchanges (DEXs), yield farming, and more. By automating these financial processes through smart contracts, DeFi eliminates the need for traditional intermediaries, such as banks or brokers, offering users greater control over their assets and financial activities.

Automated Lending and Borrowing

One of the prominent use cases of smart contracts in DeFi is automated lending and borrowing protocols. Platforms like Compound, Aave, and MakerDAO utilize smart contracts to enable users to lend their assets and earn interest or borrow assets by providing collateral. Smart contracts automatically manage loan agreements, interest rates, and collateral ratios, ensuring that lending and borrowing operations are executed seamlessly without the need for intermediaries.

Decentralized Exchanges (DEXs)

Smart contracts power decentralized exchanges, allowing users to trade digital assets directly with one another without relying on a centralized authority. Platforms like Uniswap and SushiSwap deploy smart contracts to create liquidity pools and execute trades based on predetermined rules. Users can trade assets securely, and liquidity providers earn fees for contributing assets to these decentralized liquidity pools.

Yield Farming and Liquidity Mining

Yield farming, a popular DeFi practice, involves users providing liquidity to decentralized protocols in exchange for yield or governance tokens. Smart contracts automate the distribution of rewards to liquidity providers based on predefined rules. Liquidity mining, a subset of yield farming, incentivizes users to participate actively in a DeFi ecosystem by offering additional tokens as rewards. Smart contracts play a pivotal role in managing these incentive structures and distributing rewards efficiently.

Decentralized Autonomous Organizations (DAOs)

Smart contracts are the cornerstone of decentralized autonomous organizations (DAOs), which are entities governed by code and executed on the blockchain. DAOs use smart contracts to establish rules, voting mechanisms, and governance processes that enable decentralized decision-making by token holders. DAOs have been employed for various purposes, including protocol governance, funding allocation, and community-driven initiatives within the DeFi space.

Interoperability and Composability

Smart contracts contribute to the interoperability and composability of DeFi protocols. Different decentralized applications (DApps) can interact with each other through smart contracts, creating a modular and interoperable ecosystem. This composability allows developers to build on existing protocols, combining various functionalities to create new and innovative financial products and services.

Challenges and Considerations

Despite the transformative potential of smart contracts in DeFi, challenges and considerations exist. Security vulnerabilities in smart contracts, such as coding errors or exploits, pose risks to users and funds. The decentralized and permissionless nature of DeFi also means that users must exercise caution and conduct due diligence when interacting with smart contracts. Ongoing efforts in the industry focus on enhancing the security of smart contracts through audits, bug bounties, and best practices in coding standards.

Regulatory Considerations

As DeFi continues to gain prominence, regulatory considerations surrounding smart contracts are emerging. Regulators are navigating the challenges of overseeing decentralized and automated financial systems, and the regulatory landscape for smart contracts in DeFi is evolving. Projects and platforms are increasingly exploring compliance mechanisms while striving to maintain the principles of decentralization.

Future Outlook

The integration of smart contracts in DeFi has unleashed a wave of innovation, offering users decentralized alternatives to traditional financial services. As the ecosystem continues to mature, smart contracts are likely to play a central role in shaping the future of decentralized finance. Enhancements in security, scalability, and interoperability will contribute to a more robust and user-friendly DeFi landscape, expanding the reach and impact of smart contracts in redefining the global financial system.

Decentralized Lending and Borrowing

Decentralized lending and borrowing have emerged as transformative pillars within the decentralized finance (DeFi) ecosystem, reshaping traditional financial services by providing users with alternatives to traditional lending institutions. These decentralized protocols leverage smart contracts on blockchain networks to automate lending and borrowing processes, allowing users to access and provide liquidity in a permissionless and trustless manner. The decentralized nature of these platforms eliminates the need for intermediaries, providing users with greater control over their assets and financial activities.

Decentralized Lending Protocols

Decentralized lending protocols enable users to lend their digital assets to others in exchange for interest payments. Platforms like Compound, Aave, and MakerDAO utilize smart contracts to facilitate lending activities in a decentralized manner. Users can supply their crypto assets to these protocols, which are then pooled together to create liquidity. Borrowers, on the other hand, can leverage their deposited assets as collateral to borrow other assets. Interest rates are determined algorithmically based on the supply and demand dynamics within the platform.

Automated Interest Rates and Collateralization

Smart contracts govern the calculation and distribution of interest rates on decentralized lending platforms. These interest rates are dynamically adjusted based on the utilization of assets within the platform. If a particular asset is in high demand for borrowing, its interest rate may increase to incentivize more users to supply that asset. Additionally, smart contracts manage collateralization ratios, ensuring that borrowers maintain a sufficient level of collateral to secure their loans. If the value of the collateral falls below a specified threshold, liquidation mechanisms may be triggered to protect lenders.

Decentralized Borrowing Platforms

Decentralized borrowing platforms enable users to borrow digital assets by providing collateral in the form of other digital assets. Users can access liquidity without the need for credit checks or traditional financial intermediaries. This permissionless borrowing model allows users globally, including those without access to traditional banking services, to participate in lending and borrowing activities. Platforms like Compound and Aave facilitate decentralized borrowing, providing users with flexibility and control over their borrowing strategies.

Collateralized Debt Positions (CDPs)

In systems like MakerDAO, users create Collateralized Debt Positions (CDPs) by depositing collateral, typically in the form of stablecoins or other supported assets. These CDPs generate a stablecoin called DAI, which users can borrow against their collateral. The stability of DAI is maintained through mechanisms that automatically adjust interest rates and incentivize users to adjust their positions based on market conditions. This decentralized stablecoin has gained popularity as a borrowing and lending instrument within the DeFi space.

Yield Farming and Liquidity Mining

Decentralized lending and borrowing protocols often integrate yield farming and liquidity mining incentives. Users who lend or borrow on these platforms can earn additional tokens as rewards. Yield farming involves users staking their assets within a protocol to earn governance tokens or additional assets. Liquidity mining incentivizes users to provide liquidity to specific pools, earning them additional tokens or a share of the platform's transaction fees. These mechanisms contribute to the growth and sustainability of decentralized lending and borrowing ecosystems.

Challenges and Risks

While decentralized lending and borrowing offer numerous benefits, challenges and risks exist within the DeFi space. Smart contract vulnerabilities, coding errors, and potential exploits pose risks to user funds. Platforms undergo audits and security assessments to mitigate these risks, but users must exercise caution and conduct due diligence when participating in DeFi activities. Regulatory considerations are also evolving, and the DeFi space is navigating the challenges of compliance within a decentralized framework.

Integration of Oracles

Decentralized lending and borrowing protocols often integrate oracles to bring external data onto the blockchain. Oracles provide price feeds and information about assets, enabling smart contracts to make informed decisions. Accurate and reliable oracles are essential for the proper functioning of decentralized lending platforms, as they help determine asset values and trigger events such as liquidations.

Future Developments

Decentralized lending and borrowing are dynamic fields within the broader DeFi landscape. Ongoing developments include the exploration of new collateral types, improvements in interest rate models, and the integration of novel financial instruments. As the space matures, interoperability between different lending and borrowing platforms may become more prevalent, creating a cohesive and interconnected DeFi ecosystem.

Challenges and Opportunities in DeFi

Decentralized Finance (DeFi) has emerged as a disruptive force in the financial industry, offering a decentralized alternative to traditional banking and financial services. While DeFi presents numerous opportunities, it also faces various challenges that need to be addressed for sustained growth and widespread adoption.

In navigating the challenges and opportunities within the DeFi space, ongoing collaboration between developers, regulators, and users is crucial. Addressing security concerns, improving user experience, and finding scalable solutions are essential steps to realizing the full potential of decentralized finance. As the ecosystem matures, DeFi has the potential to redefine traditional financial systems, providing a decentralized, inclusive, and programmable alternative for users worldwide.

Challenges

Security Concerns

One of the primary challenges in DeFi is the vulnerability to smart contract exploits and hacks. The decentralized and open-source nature of DeFi platforms makes them attractive targets for malicious actors. Several high-profile security incidents have raised concerns about the robustness of smart contracts and the overall security of DeFi protocols.

Regulatory Uncertainty

The regulatory landscape for DeFi is still evolving, and there is a lack of clarity on how existing financial regulations apply to decentralized systems. Regulatory uncertainty poses challenges for DeFi projects, potentially hindering their development and adoption. Striking a balance between innovation and regulatory compliance is a complex task for the DeFi space.

Scalability

As DeFi platforms gain popularity, scalability becomes a critical issue. Blockchain networks, particularly Ethereum, which hosts a significant portion of DeFi projects, face scalability challenges, leading to congestion and high transaction fees during peak usage times. Scalability solutions are actively being explored to address these issues and enhance the overall user experience.

User Experience

DeFi platforms often have a steeper learning curve for non-technical users. The complexity of interacting with decentralized applications (DApps), managing private keys, and navigating through different protocols can be intimidating. Improving the user experience is crucial for broader DeFi adoption, requiring user-friendly interfaces and educational resources.

Volatility and Market Risks

DeFi tokens and assets are often subject to high volatility, presenting risks for both lenders and borrowers. Fluctuations in asset prices can lead to liquidations, affecting collateralized positions. Managing and mitigating these market risks is essential for the stability and sustainability of decentralized lending and borrowing platforms.

Opportunities

Financial Inclusion

DeFi has the potential to bring financial services to underserved populations globally. By operating on blockchain networks, DeFi platforms can provide financial services without the need for traditional banking infrastructure, offering an inclusive financial ecosystem accessible to anyone with an internet connection.

Permissionless Innovation

The permissionless nature of DeFi allows for rapid innovation and experimentation. Developers can create and deploy financial applications without seeking approval from intermediaries, fostering a dynamic ecosystem where new ideas and protocols can be tested and implemented quickly.

Decentralized Exchanges (DEXs)

The rise of decentralized exchanges is a significant opportunity within DeFi. DEXs, such as Uniswap and SushiSwap, enable users to trade digital assets directly from their wallets without relying on centralized exchanges. This contributes to greater liquidity and resilience against single points of failure.

Programmable Money

DeFi introduces the concept of programmable money through smart contracts. Users can automate financial transactions, lending, borrowing, and other financial activities without the need for intermediaries. This programmability opens new possibilities for creating complex financial instruments and services.

Yield Farming and Liquidity Mining

DeFi platforms often incentivize users through yield farming and liquidity mining. Users can earn additional tokens by providing liquidity to various protocols. These incentives attract liquidity, contributing to the growth of DeFi ecosystems and rewarding active participants.

Decentralized Autonomous Organizations (DAOs)

DAOs represent an opportunity for decentralized governance within DeFi projects. Token holders can participate in decision-making processes, including protocol upgrades, changes to parameters, and fund allocations. This democratic governance model enhances community involvement and ownership.

Interoperability

DeFi projects have the opportunity to enhance interoperability between different blockchain networks. The ability to seamlessly transfer assets and data between diverse DeFi protocols and blockchains contributes to a more interconnected and collaborative ecosystem.

V. Tokenization of Assets

Tokenizing Real-world Assets (Real Estate, Art, etc.)

Tokenizing real-world assets, such as real estate, art, and other tangible assets, has emerged as a transformative application of blockchain technology within the broader realm of decentralized finance (DeFi). This process involves representing ownership of physical assets through digital tokens on a blockchain, allowing for increased liquidity, fractional ownership, and seamless transferability. The tokenization of real-world assets has the potential to democratize access to traditionally illiquid markets and redefine the way individuals invest in and interact with tangible assets.

Real Estate Tokenization

Real estate tokenization involves converting ownership rights of physical properties into digital tokens on a blockchain. Each token represents a fraction of the property, allowing investors to own a portion of the real estate asset. This fractional ownership model makes real estate investments more accessible to a broader range of investors, as they can participate with smaller amounts of capital. Platforms facilitating real estate tokenization aim to streamline the investment process, enhance liquidity, and reduce barriers to entry in the real estate market.

Art Tokenization

Tokenizing art involves creating digital tokens that represent ownership or shares of an artwork. These tokens can be bought, sold, and traded on blockchain platforms, providing investors with exposure to the art market without the need to physically own the artwork. Art tokenization introduces a new way for art enthusiasts and investors to engage with the art world, enabling fractional ownership, increased liquidity, and the ability to diversify art portfolios.

Benefits of Tokenizing Real-world Assets

Liquidity and Fractional Ownership

Tokenization of real-world assets enhances liquidity by enabling fractional ownership. Investors can buy and sell fractions of assets, allowing them to access markets that were traditionally illiquid due to high entry costs or limited investment opportunities.

Global Accessibility

Blockchain-based tokenization provides a borderless platform for investors worldwide to participate in real-world asset markets. This global accessibility opens up investment opportunities to a broader audience, breaking down geographical barriers and fostering a more inclusive financial landscape.

24/7 Trading and Settlement

Tokenized assets trade on blockchain networks, which operate 24/7. This contrasts with traditional financial markets that have specific trading hours. The continuous availability of tokenized assets for trading and settlement enhances market efficiency and responsiveness to market dynamics.

Reduced Friction and Costs

The use of blockchain technology streamlines the issuance, transfer, and management of tokenized assets, reducing the need for intermediaries and associated transaction costs. This increased efficiency benefits both issuers and investors by minimizing administrative overhead and facilitating quicker, cost-effective transactions.

Automated Compliance

Smart contracts embedded in tokenized assets can enforce compliance with regulatory requirements. By automating compliance features, such as investor accreditation and restrictions on secondary market trading, tokenization platforms aim to enhance regulatory adherence within the decentralized finance space.

Challenges and Considerations

Regulatory Landscape

The regulatory environment for tokenized real-world assets is still evolving. Issuers and investors need to navigate regulatory frameworks to ensure compliance with existing laws. Regulatory clarity is crucial for widespread adoption and investor confidence in tokenized assets.

Security and Custody

Ensuring the security of digital assets and private keys is paramount in the tokenization of real-world assets. Platforms must implement robust security measures to protect against hacks and unauthorized access. Additionally, the question of custody for physical assets represented by digital tokens requires careful consideration.

Market Liquidity

While tokenization aims to enhance liquidity, the actual liquidity of tokenized assets depends on market demand. The success of tokenized real-world assets in secondary markets relies on the ability to attract a diverse pool of investors and create active trading environments.

Asset Valuation

Determining the fair market value of tokenized assets, especially unique or illiquid ones like art, can pose challenges. Establishing transparent and standardized valuation methods is essential for investor confidence and market credibility.

Educational Awareness

Educating investors about the concept of tokenizing real-world assets and the technicalities of blockchain technology is crucial for fostering adoption. Increased awareness and understanding will contribute to the acceptance and integration of tokenized assets into traditional investment portfolios.

Future Outlook

The tokenization of real-world assets represents a significant evolution in the financial landscape, offering new avenues for investment and democratizing access to traditionally exclusive markets. As the regulatory environment matures, technological advancements address security concerns, and market infrastructure develops, tokenized real-world assets are poised to play a prominent role in the broader adoption of decentralized finance. The ongoing exploration of use cases beyond real estate and art, including tokenizing commodities, intellectual property, and more, further expands the potential of blockchain-based asset tokenization in reshaping the future of finance.

Security Tokens and Regulatory Compliance

Security tokens, a subset of digital tokens, represent ownership in real-world assets and are subject to securities regulations. Unlike utility tokens, which grant access to a product or service, security tokens derive their value from external, tradable assets and fall under regulatory frameworks governing securities. The intersection of security tokens and regulatory compliance is a critical aspect of the broader decentralized finance (DeFi) landscape, as it aims to bring transparency, investor protection, and legal legitimacy to the tokenization of assets.

Regulatory Compliance for Security Tokens

Security tokens operate within existing securities regulations, which vary across jurisdictions. These regulations are designed to protect investors by ensuring transparency, disclosure of material information, and adherence to specific processes for issuing, trading, and transferring ownership of securities. Issuers of security tokens must comply with these regulations to maintain legal legitimacy and protect the interests of investors.

Legal Frameworks and Jurisdictional Variances

Different countries have distinct regulatory frameworks for securities, and the treatment of security tokens varies accordingly. Some jurisdictions have well-defined regulations that explicitly address digital securities, while others are in the process of adapting existing securities laws to encompass the evolving landscape of blockchain-based assets. Navigating these jurisdictional variances is a complex task for issuers, investors, and regulators seeking to strike a balance between fostering innovation and ensuring investor protection.

KYC (Know Your Customer) and AML (Anti-Money Laundering)

Security token offerings (STOs) typically require robust Know Your Customer (KYC) and Anti-Money Laundering (AML) procedures. These measures are implemented to verify the identities of investors, assess their eligibility to participate, and mitigate the risk of illicit activities. KYC and AML compliance contribute to the legitimacy of security token offerings and help prevent fraudulent activities within the decentralized finance space.

Accredited Investor Requirements

In many jurisdictions, the issuance and trading of security tokens are limited to accredited investors. Accredited investors are individuals or entities that meet specific financial criteria, demonstrating a level of sophistication and ability to understand the risks associated with investing in securities. This restriction aims to protect retail investors from the potentially higher risks associated with certain types of securities.

Smart Contracts for Regulatory Compliance

Smart contracts, self-executing code on a blockchain, can be programmed to enforce compliance with regulatory requirements. These programmable contracts automate various aspects of the security token lifecycle, such as investor accreditation, transfer restrictions, and compliance reporting. By embedding compliance features in smart contracts, issuers can enhance transparency and streamline regulatory adherence within the decentralized financial ecosystem.

Regulatory Challenges and Evolving Standards

The regulatory landscape for security tokens is still evolving, and challenges persist in achieving global standardization. Regulatory bodies are actively engaging with industry stakeholders to establish clear guidelines and standards for the issuance and trading of security tokens. The development of harmonized standards across jurisdictions is crucial for fostering confidence in security tokens and encouraging broader market participation.

Security Token Exchanges and Market Infrastructure

The emergence of security token exchanges is a key development in the ecosystem, providing platforms for the issuance, trading, and secondary market liquidity of security tokens. These exchanges play a pivotal role in ensuring that security tokens adhere to regulatory standards and compliance measures. Establishing robust market infrastructure, including licensed and regulated exchanges, contributes to the legitimacy and long-term viability of security tokens.

Cross-Border Compliance and Regulatory Coordination

Security tokens often involve cross-border transactions, requiring coordination between regulatory authorities to address jurisdictional challenges. Regulatory bodies worldwide are exploring ways to collaborate and harmonize their approaches to facilitate cross-border compliance for security token offerings. Initiatives aimed at fostering regulatory coordination will contribute to the global acceptance and integration of security tokens into traditional financial markets.

Future Outlook

The integration of security tokens and regulatory compliance is a dynamic and ongoing process. As regulatory frameworks continue to evolve and mature, security tokens have the potential to become a mainstream financial instrument, offering benefits such as increased liquidity, fractional ownership, and streamlined settlement processes. Industry collaboration, regulatory clarity, and technological innovations will shape the future of security tokens, paving the way for a compliant and transparent tokenized securities market within the decentralized finance ecosystem.

NFTs (Non-Fungible Tokens) and Their Impact on Digital Ownership

Non-Fungible Tokens (NFTs) have emerged as a revolutionary force in the digital realm, transforming the concept of ownership and value in the digital space. NFTs are unique, indivisible tokens that represent ownership or proof of authenticity for a specific digital or physical asset. Most associated with digital art, NFTs have broadened their scope to encompass various digital and tangible assets, including music, videos, virtual real estate, and even real-world assets. The impact of

NFTs on digital ownership is profound, introducing new possibilities for creators, collectors, and the broader creative economy.

The future trends in tokenization point toward a more interconnected, efficient, and inclusive global financial ecosystem. As blockchain technology matures and regulatory frameworks evolve, tokenization is set to become a transformative force, impacting not only the financial industry but a broad spectrum of sectors, redefining how we perceive and interact with ownership in the digital age.

Unique Digital Ownership

NFTs provide a mechanism for establishing true ownership and authenticity in the digital realm. Unlike traditional digital files, which can be easily copied and shared, NFTs are stored on blockchain networks, providing an immutable and transparent record of ownership. This unique aspect ensures that the owner of an NFT holds the genuine and original version of the associated digital asset.

Empowering Digital Creators

NFTs have empowered digital creators by enabling them to monetize their work directly. Artists, musicians, and content creators can mint their creations as NFTs, allowing them to retain control over their intellectual property and receive direct compensation from buyers. This shift in the paradigm of digital ownership decentralizes the creative economy, reducing reliance on intermediaries and providing creators with a more direct and equitable relationship with their audience.

Digital Scarcity and Value

NFTs introduce the concept of digital scarcity, imbuing digital assets with a sense of rarity and uniqueness. This scarcity is achieved through the use of blockchain technology, which ensures that each NFT is distinct and cannot be replicated. The perceived scarcity contributes to the perceived value of digital assets, creating a market where collectors are willing to pay a premium for ownership of a one-of-a-kind digital item.

Tokenization of Tangible Assets

Beyond the digital realm, NFTs have expanded into the tokenization of tangible assets. Real-world assets, such as real estate, luxury goods, and even portions of physical artworks, can be represented as NFTs. This tokenization of tangible assets opens new avenues for fractional ownership and trading in traditional markets, bringing the benefits of blockchain technology to the broader spectrum of asset classes.

Decentralized Ownership and Interoperability

NFTs operate on blockchain networks, promoting decentralized ownership and eliminating the need for centralized authorities to validate or transfer ownership. Interoperability between different blockchain platforms allows NFTs to be transferred and traded across various ecosystems, enhancing liquidity, and providing users with greater flexibility in managing their digital assets.

Challenges and Considerations

Despite the transformative impact, NFTs face challenges and considerations. Environmental concerns related to the energy consumption of certain blockchain networks used for NFT transactions have sparked debates within the community. Additionally, issues related to copyright infringement, plagiarism, and the need for clearer intellectual property frameworks in the NFT space are ongoing challenges that require attention.

Cultural and Societal Impacts

NFTs have cultural and societal implications by redefining the relationship between creators and consumers. The ability to directly support and engage with creators fosters a sense of community and patronage. Digital ownership through NFTs also challenges traditional notions of value and ownership, raising questions about the nature of art, collectibles, and the perceived value of digital assets in the digital age.

Future of NFTs and Digital Ownership

The future of NFTs and digital ownership holds tremendous potential for further innovation and integration into various industries. Continued advancements in blockchain technology, scalability solutions to address environmental concerns, and the development of decentralized identity solutions will contribute to the maturation of the NFT space. As NFTs continue to evolve, they are likely to play a central role in shaping the future of digital ownership, transforming the way individuals perceive, create, and exchange value in the digital landscape. The impact of NFTs extends beyond the realm of art and collectibles, influencing the broader digital economy and contributing to the ongoing paradigm shift in the concept of ownership.

Future Trends in Tokenization

The future of tokenization holds promising trends that extend beyond the current applications, presenting opportunities for widespread adoption and transformative changes across various industries. As blockchain technology matures, here are some anticipated trends in the evolution of tokenization:

Cross-Asset Tokenization

Future trends in tokenization suggest an expansion beyond the current focus on digital assets. Traditional assets like real estate, stocks, bonds, and commodities are likely to undergo tokenization, enabling fractional ownership and increasing liquidity in markets that were historically illiquid. This cross-asset tokenization could bridge the gap between traditional financial markets and the blockchain-based decentralized financial ecosystem.

Enhanced Regulatory Clarity

Regulatory clarity is crucial for the widespread adoption of tokenization. Future trends indicate that regulatory bodies will provide clearer guidelines for the issuance, trading, and management of tokenized assets. Governments and regulatory agencies are likely to collaborate to establish comprehensive frameworks that balance innovation with investor protection, fostering a conducive environment for tokenization to thrive.

Integration of Smart Contracts

Smart contracts, self-executing pieces of code on a blockchain, will play an increasingly integral role in tokenization. The future will witness the development of more sophisticated smart contracts that automate complex processes, such as revenue-sharing agreements, dividend distributions, and compliance enforcement. This will enhance the efficiency and transparency of tokenized ecosystems.

Tokenization of Intellectual Property

Beyond tangible assets, the tokenization of intellectual property, including patents, copyrights, and trademarks, is anticipated to gain traction. This trend could revolutionize how creators and innovators monetize their intellectual assets, allowing for more direct and efficient compensation through tokenized ownership and licensing.

Interoperability Across Blockchains

As the blockchain space continues to evolve, interoperability between different blockchain networks will become increasingly crucial. Future trends in tokenization suggest the development of protocols and standards that facilitate seamless transferability and trading of tokens across various blockchains. This interoperability will contribute to a more connected and collaborative decentralized ecosystem.

Environmental Considerations and Sustainable Tokenization

Given the growing concern over the environmental impact of certain blockchain networks, the future of tokenization will likely witness an emphasis on sustainable practices. The development and adoption of eco-friendly consensus mechanisms and energy-efficient blockchain networks will address environmental concerns, making tokenization more socially responsible.

Tokenized Identities and Decentralized Identity Solutions

The future of tokenization includes the tokenization of identities, where individuals can have verifiable and portable digital identities represented by tokens. Decentralized identity solutions aim to give users control over their personal information and reduce reliance on centralized identity providers, enhancing privacy and security in the digital world.

Tokenized Securities and Institutional Adoption

The tokenization of securities is poised to gain momentum, with traditional financial institutions exploring ways to leverage blockchain technology for issuing and managing tokenized securities. Institutional adoption of tokenization will bring legitimacy and significant liquidity to tokenized markets, opening new avenues for both retail and institutional investors.

Non-Fungible Tokens (NFTs) Beyond Digital Art

While NFTs have gained widespread attention in the realm of digital art, future trends suggest that NFTs will extend beyond the art world. Tokenization of real-world assets, virtual goods, and in-game assets within the gaming industry is likely to witness substantial growth. NFTs may become integral to the ownership and trading of unique items across various virtual and augmented reality platforms.

Continued Innovation in DeFi

The decentralized finance (DeFi) space will continue to be a hotbed for innovation in tokenization. Future trends include the development of more sophisticated decentralized applications (DApps), decentralized exchanges, and decentralized autonomous organizations (DAOs) that leverage tokenization to create novel financial instruments and services.

VI. Central Bank Digital Currencies (CBDCs)

Introduction to CBDCs

Central Bank Digital Currencies (CBDCs) represent a significant evolution in the realm of digital finance, offering a form of digital currency issued and regulated by a central bank. As the digitalization of financial systems accelerates, CBDCs have emerged as a focal point for central banks worldwide, exploring the potential benefits and challenges associated with the issuance of sovereign-backed digital currencies. The introduction of CBDCs reflects a fundamental shift in the concept of money, as it moves from physical cash and traditional forms of electronic money to a digital representation of national currency.

The introduction of CBDCs marks a pivotal moment in the evolution of money and finance. As central banks navigate the technological, regulatory, and economic complexities associated with CBDCs, the impact on the global financial landscape is expected to be substantial. The ongoing exploration and implementation of CBDCs signify a commitment to adapting to the digital age while addressing the challenges and opportunities that come with the transformation of traditional monetary systems.

Definition and Nature of CBDCs

A CBDC is a digital version of a country's national currency, backed by the central bank and recognized as a legal tender. Unlike existing forms of digital currency, such as bank deposits or electronic payment systems, CBDCs are directly issued by the central bank and are considered a liability of the central bank on its balance sheet. CBDCs can exist in two main forms: retail CBDCs, which are accessible to the public, and wholesale CBDCs, designed for use by financial institutions in interbank transactions.

Motivations for CBDCs

Central banks around the world are exploring CBDCs for various reasons. One primary motivation is to adapt to the changing landscape of payments and finance in the digital era. The rise of private cryptocurrencies, changing consumer preferences, and the potential impact on monetary policy have spurred central banks to investigate CBDCs as a means of maintaining control over their currency and payment systems. CBDCs also offer the potential for greater financial inclusion, as they can provide a secure and accessible form of digital currency to a wider population.

Key Features of CBDCs

CBDCs share several key features that distinguish them from other forms of digital currency. These features include:

Central Bank Backing

CBDCs are directly issued and regulated by the central bank, providing them with a level of trust and stability inherent in traditional fiat currencies.

Legal Tender Status

CBDCs are recognized as legal tender, meaning they can be used for all transactions, public and private, just like physical cash.

Accessibility

Depending on the design, CBDCs can be accessible to the public or limited to financial institutions for specific use cases. Retail CBDCs aim to provide a digital counterpart to physical cash, while wholesale CBDCs facilitate interbank settlements.

Traceability and Control

CBDCs offer central banks enhanced traceability of transactions, providing insights into the flow of money within the economy. This feature can enable better control over monetary policy and mitigate illicit activities.

Interest-Bearing

CBDCs can be designed to bear interest, providing additional monetary policy tools for central banks to manage economic conditions.

Challenges and Considerations

Despite the potential benefits, the introduction of CBDCs comes with various challenges and considerations. These include:

Technological Infrastructure

The development and implementation of robust technological infrastructure to support CBDCs is a significant undertaking for central banks. Scalability, security, and interoperability are key factors in ensuring the smooth functioning of CBDC systems.

Privacy Concerns

The traceability and transparency features of CBDCs raise privacy concerns. Striking a balance between privacy and regulatory oversight is a complex challenge that central banks must navigate.

Impact on Commercial Banks

The widespread adoption of CBDCs could potentially impact the traditional role of commercial banks, as depositors may opt to hold CBDCs directly with the central bank instead of using commercial bank accounts.

Cross-Border Implications

Coordination and cooperation between central banks will be essential to address potential cross-border challenges associated with CBDCs, including regulatory harmonization and interoperability.

Cybersecurity Risks

The digital nature of CBDCs exposes them to cybersecurity risks. Central banks must implement robust security measures to protect against cyber threats and unauthorized access.

Global Trends and Pilots

Several countries have actively explored CBDCs, with some launching pilot programs to test their feasibility. China has been at the forefront of CBDC development, conducting trials in various cities and rolling out the Digital Currency Electronic Payment (DCEP) system. Other countries, including the European Union, the United States, and various nations in Asia and the Middle East, have initiated research or pilot programs to explore the potential of CBDCs in their respective economies.

Motivations for CBDCs

The motivations for Central Bank Digital Currencies (CBDCs) are rooted in the rapidly evolving landscape of digital finance, where technological advancements and changing consumer preferences have prompted central banks worldwide to explore the issuance of sovereign-backed digital currencies. Several key motivations underpin the development and consideration of CBDCs, each driven by a combination of economic, technological, and regulatory factors.

The motivations for CBDCs reflect a multifaceted response to the changing dynamics of the digital economy. As central banks navigate the complexities of technological integration, regulatory considerations, and societal needs, the development and issuance of CBDCs represent a proactive approach to modernizing the financial infrastructure. The motivations go beyond mere adaptation to digital trends; they encompass a broader vision of promoting financial inclusion, efficiency, and stability in a digital-first world.

Digitalization of Payments

The shift towards a cashless society and the increasing prevalence of digital payment methods have been significant motivations for CBDCs. As traditional forms of money, including physical cash, face competition from private digital currencies and electronic payment systems, central banks recognize the need to adapt to the digital era. CBDCs aim to provide a secure and efficient digital alternative to physical cash, ensuring that central banks maintain control over the payment systems within their jurisdictions.

Competition with Private Cryptocurrencies

The rise of private cryptocurrencies, such as Bitcoin and other decentralized digital assets, has spurred central banks to consider CBDCs as a response to the changing dynamics of the financial landscape. While private cryptocurrencies offer certain advantages, including borderless transactions and pseudonymous ownership, they also present challenges related to volatility, regulatory concerns, and potential threats to financial stability. CBDCs provide central banks with a means to offer a digital currency that combines the benefits of innovation with the stability and regulatory oversight of traditional fiat currencies.

Financial Inclusion

CBDCs have the potential to enhance financial inclusion by providing a secure and accessible digital currency to a broader segment of the population. In many economies, a significant portion of the population remains unbanked or underbanked, lacking access to basic financial services. CBDCs, designed with inclusivity in mind, could facilitate greater participation in the formal financial system, reducing reliance on physical cash and promoting economic participation among marginalized communities.

Monetary Policy Tools

CBDCs offer central banks additional tools for implementing monetary policy. The programmable nature of digital currencies allows central banks to implement interest-bearing CBDCs, enabling them to influence spending patterns and economic activity more directly. This feature could enhance the effectiveness of monetary policy in response to economic challenges such as inflation, deflation, or economic downturns.

Reduction of Cash-Related Costs

The management and circulation of physical cash incur significant costs for central banks and financial institutions. Printing, transporting, and securing physical currency involve expenses that could be mitigated by transitioning to a digital currency system. CBDCs, as a digital form of central bank money, have the potential to reduce the costs associated with the production and distribution of physical cash.

Strengthening Regulatory Oversight

CBDCs provide a tool for enhancing regulatory oversight in the financial system. The traceability and transparency feature inherent in blockchain technology, which underlies many CBDC implementations, can offer regulators greater insights into financial transactions. This increased visibility enables more effective monitoring of money laundering, fraud, and other illicit activities, contributing to the overall integrity of the financial system.

Technological Innovation

The exploration and adoption of CBDCs represents a commitment to embracing technological innovation within the financial sector. By leveraging blockchain technology and other advancements, central banks can create digital currencies that are not only secure and efficient but also capable of integrating seamlessly with emerging financial technologies. This emphasis on innovation positions central banks at the forefront of shaping the future of digital finance.

Impact on Traditional Banking

The advent of Central Bank Digital Currencies (CBDCs) poses a multifaceted impact on traditional banking, reshaping the financial landscape and challenging established norms. As central banks globally explore the development of digital currencies, several key areas within traditional banking are likely to be influenced by the introduction of CBDCs.

The impact of CBDCs on traditional banking is profound and multifaceted. While CBDCs bring opportunities for increased efficiency, financial inclusion, and technological innovation, they also pose challenges to traditional banking structures, deposit models, and intermediation roles. Traditional banks are faced with the imperative to adapt their strategies, embrace technological advancements, and collaborate within a changing financial landscape where CBDCs play a central role in shaping the future of money and payments.

Transformation of Payment Systems

CBDCs have the potential to revolutionize payment systems by providing a direct digital alternative to physical cash. This transformation could impact traditional banking services, particularly in terms of payment processing and settlement. With the ability to settle transactions in real-time and operate 24/7, CBDCs could reduce the reliance on traditional banking payment rails, leading to increased efficiency and faster settlement times.

Evolution of Deposit Structures

The introduction of CBDCs may prompt changes in deposit structures within traditional banks. As individuals and businesses opt for CBDCs as a form of digital currency, the demand for traditional bank deposits may shift. The appeal of CBDCs lies in their direct issuance by central banks, providing a secure and interest-bearing digital form of money. Traditional banks may need to adapt their deposit offerings to remain competitive in this changing landscape.

Impact on Intermediation Role

Traditional banks play a crucial role as intermediaries in the financial system, facilitating lending and borrowing activities. The advent of CBDCs could influence this intermediation role by offering an alternative form of digital currency directly issued by the central bank. This direct access to central bank money may impact the traditional fractional reserve banking model and challenge the intermediation services provided by commercial banks.

Changes in Interest Rate Dynamics

The implementation of CBDCs could impact the traditional mechanisms through which central banks implement monetary policy, particularly in the context of interest rates. The programmable nature of CBDCs allows central banks to implement negative interest rates more effectively, influencing spending behavior and economic activity. This shift in interest rate dynamics may require traditional banks to adjust their strategies to navigate a landscape where negative interest rates are more readily implemented.

5. Technological Innovation and Collaboration

The integration of CBDCs requires significant technological innovation, and traditional banks must adapt to stay competitive. Embracing blockchain technology, ensuring cybersecurity measures, and developing user-friendly interfaces become imperative for traditional banks to remain relevant in a CBDC-driven ecosystem. Collaboration between central banks, financial institutions, and technology providers will be essential to navigate the complexities of implementing and maintaining CBDC infrastructure.

6. Enhanced Regulatory Oversight

The traceability and transparency feature inherent in CBDCs offer regulators greater visibility into financial transactions. This enhanced regulatory oversight can be a positive development for traditional banks, as it aids in monitoring and preventing illicit activities such as money laundering and fraud. However, it also means that banks need to ensure compliance with evolving regulatory frameworks associated with CBDCs.

7. Competition and Innovation Pressure

CBDCs introduce a new form of digital currency directly issued by central banks, providing consumers and businesses with an alternative to traditional bank deposits. This increased competition for deposits may place pressure on traditional banks to innovate their services, enhance customer experience, and offer value-added features to retain their customer base in the face of the evolving digital currency landscape.

8. Financial Inclusion Initiatives

CBDCs have the potential to promote financial inclusion by providing a secure and accessible digital currency. Traditional banks may need to collaborate with central banks to ensure that CBDCs complement existing banking services and contribute to inclusive financial ecosystems. This collaboration can involve leveraging CBDCs to reach unbanked or underbanked populations, expanding the scope of financial services.

Global Perspectives on CBDCs

Central Bank Digital Currencies (CBDCs) have garnered widespread attention and consideration on the global stage, with central banks across different countries exploring the potential implementation of digital currencies. The perspectives on CBDCs vary, reflecting the diverse economic, technological, and regulatory landscapes of nations around the world.

The global perspectives on CBDCs reflect a dynamic and evolving landscape where central banks navigate the complexities of digital finance. While motivations for CBDC adoption vary, the common thread lies in the recognition of digital currencies as a transformative force with the potential to reshape payments, enhance financial inclusion, and address challenges posed by evolving financial technologies. As central banks collaborate, conduct trials, and share insights, the future of CBDCs continues to unfold, offering both opportunities and challenges in the quest for a digital future of money.

Asia-Pacific Region

Several countries in the Asia-Pacific region have been at the forefront of CBDC development and adoption. China, with its Digital Currency Electronic Payment (DCEP) project, has emerged as a trailblazer, conducting extensive pilots and trials. Other nations, such as Japan and South Korea, have also initiated research and pilot programs to explore the feasibility of CBDCs. The region's focus on CBDCs is often linked to the rapid digitalization of payments, technological innovation, and the desire to maintain control over domestic monetary systems.

European Union

Within the European Union (EU), CBDC discussions have gained momentum, with the European Central Bank (ECB) actively exploring the concept. The EU's approach emphasizes the potential benefits of CBDCs in terms of financial innovation, cross-border payments, and the potential to address challenges posed by private digital currencies. However, considerations regarding data privacy, cybersecurity, and the potential impact on traditional banking structures remain central to the EU's deliberations on CBDCs.

North America

In North America, both the United States and Canada have been engaged in discussions and research on CBDCs, albeit with different paces and approaches. The U.S. Federal Reserve has taken a cautious stance, emphasizing the need for careful evaluation and public consultation before making any decisions on CBDC issuance. Canada, on the other hand, has been exploring the potential benefits of CBDCs, including their role in supporting a more resilient and efficient payments ecosystem.

Emerging Markets

Emerging markets, particularly those facing challenges related to financial inclusion, have shown a keen interest in CBDCs. The potential to provide secure and accessible digital currency to unbanked or underbanked populations aligns with the financial inclusion objectives of many developing economies. Countries in Africa, Latin America, and Southeast Asia are exploring CBDCs as a means to address issues of financial accessibility, reduce transaction costs, and enhance the efficiency of their financial systems.

Middle East and Africa

Countries in the Middle East, such as the United Arab Emirates and Saudi Arabia, have embarked on CBDC projects to harness the potential benefits of digital currencies. These nations are motivated by a desire to enhance cross-border payments, improve financial infrastructure, and position themselves at the forefront of financial innovation. In Africa, CBDCs are seen as a tool to promote financial inclusion and overcome challenges associated with traditional banking in remote areas.

Global Collaborations and Initiatives

The global landscape of CBDCs includes collaborative efforts and initiatives. Organizations such as the International Monetary Fund (IMF) and the Bank for International Settlements (BIS) play roles in fostering discussions, research, and knowledge sharing on CBDCs. Collaborative projects aim to address common challenges, ensure interoperability between CBDCs, and establish international standards for the potential future integration of digital currencies.

Considerations and Challenges

Global perspectives on CBDCs are shaped by common considerations and challenges. Key among these are concerns related to privacy, security, interoperability, and the potential impact on traditional banking structures. Central banks worldwide grapple with finding the right balance between innovation and stability, navigating the complexities of technological integration, and addressing the regulatory implications of CBDCs.

International Monetary System Implications

The introduction of CBDCs has implications for the international monetary system. The potential for CBDCs to facilitate cross-border transactions more efficiently has led to discussions on their role in reshaping the global payments landscape. Questions regarding the potential use of CBDCs as a reserve currency or their impact on the international role of existing currencies remain subjects of exploration and debate.

VII. Cryptocurrency and the Future of Money

Cryptocurrency as a Store of Value

Cryptocurrency's role as a store of value has been a topic of significant debate and exploration, particularly with the emergence of Bitcoin as a pioneer in the digital currency space. Traditionally, stores of value have included assets like gold and other precious metals, which retain value over time and serve as a hedge against inflation. Cryptocurrencies, particularly Bitcoin, have sought to fulfill a similar function in the digital realm.

The concept of cryptocurrency as a store of value represents a paradigm shift in the way individuals and institutions perceive and preserve wealth. While challenges and debates persist, the growing acceptance and integration of cryptocurrencies into the broader financial landscape indicate that their role as stores of value will continue to be a subject of exploration and adaptation in the evolving world of finance.

Bitcoin as Digital Gold

Bitcoin, often referred to as "digital gold," has positioned itself as a decentralized and finite digital asset with properties akin to precious metals. Its capped supply of 21 million coins, enforced by its underlying blockchain technology, creates scarcity—a key characteristic of traditional stores of value. This scarcity, combined with Bitcoin's decentralized nature and robust security, has led proponents to view it as a digital store of value, analogous to gold in the physical world.

Hedging Against Inflation

One of the motivations behind considering cryptocurrencies as a store of value is their potential to serve as a hedge against inflation.

Traditional fiat currencies can be susceptible to devaluation over time due to factors such as government policies, economic instability, and excessive money printing. Cryptocurrencies, with their fixed supplies and decentralized structures, are perceived by some as a way to preserve value in an environment where traditional stores of value might face challenges.

Trust in Decentralization

The decentralized nature of cryptocurrencies contributes to their appeal as stores of value. Unlike traditional assets that may rely on centralized authorities, cryptocurrencies operate on decentralized blockchain networks. This decentralization fosters trust by eliminating the need for intermediaries and reducing the risk of manipulation or control by a single entity. Users place trust in the cryptographic principles and consensus mechanisms that underpin cryptocurrencies, enhancing their perception as reliable stores of value.

Volatility and Risk Perception

While some view cryptocurrencies as a store of value, others express reservations due to their inherent volatility. The price fluctuations witnessed in the cryptocurrency market can be substantial, leading to concerns about their ability to retain stable value over time. The volatile nature of cryptocurrencies introduces an element of risk that contrasts with the stability traditionally associated with stores of value like gold. Ongoing debates center on whether the volatility is a temporary feature or a fundamental characteristic of cryptocurrencies.

Portfolio Diversification

Cryptocurrencies are increasingly considered as a component of diversified investment portfolios. Investors seeking to diversify their holdings often explore alternative assets, including cryptocurrencies, to mitigate risk and enhance potential returns. By including cryptocurrencies in a portfolio alongside traditional assets, investors aim to achieve a balance that leverages the unique characteristics of digital assets while diversifying exposure to different types of markets.

Evolving Perception and Institutional Adoption

The perception of cryptocurrencies as stores of value has evolved over time, driven in part by growing institutional interest. High-profile endorsements, regulatory clarity, and the entry of institutional investors into the cryptocurrency market have contributed to a shift in perception. Institutions seeking to hedge against economic uncertainties and diversify their portfolios have allocated funds to cryptocurrencies, further legitimizing the idea of digital assets as stores of value.

Store of Value Competition

The landscape of stores of value is dynamic and competitive, with various assets vying for investor confidence. Gold, real estate, and government bonds have long held positions as traditional stores of value. Cryptocurrencies, as a relatively new entrant, face competition in establishing themselves as trusted and enduring assets for wealth preservation. The ongoing competition contributes to the evolution of the broader financial ecosystem.

Long-Term Viability and Future Developments

The debate around cryptocurrencies as stores of value extends to questions about their long-term viability and the impact of future developments. Technological advancements, regulatory developments, and shifts in market dynamics all play a role in shaping the future of cryptocurrencies. Ongoing research and innovation within the crypto space aim to address challenges, enhance scalability, and further solidify the role of digital assets as stores of value.

Challenges and Solutions for Mass Adoption

The mass adoption of cryptocurrencies faces several challenges that span technological, regulatory, and societal dimensions. Overcoming these obstacles is crucial for establishing cryptocurrencies as mainstream tools for financial transactions and wealth management. While the challenges for mass adoption of cryptocurrencies are substantial, ongoing innovation, regulatory collaboration, and community efforts are driving solutions. As the industry addresses scalability, regulatory clarity, security concerns, and user experience, cryptocurrencies are positioned to play a more significant role in mainstream finance, offering individuals and businesses new opportunities for financial inclusion, efficiency, and innovation.

Scalability and Transaction Speed

One of the primary technical challenges hindering mass adoption is the scalability of blockchain networks. As more users participate, transaction speeds may decrease, and fees could rise. Bitcoin, for instance, has faced scalability issues, leading to slower transaction confirmations during periods of high demand. Solutions such as layer-2 scaling solutions, like the Lightning Network for Bitcoin, aim to alleviate these challenges by facilitating faster and more cost-effective transactions off the main blockchain.

Regulatory Uncertainty

The regulatory landscape for cryptocurrencies varies significantly across different jurisdictions, creating uncertainty for businesses and users. Clarity and consistent regulations are essential for mass adoption, as they provide a legal framework that fosters trust and encourages participation. Collaboration between the cryptocurrency industry and regulatory bodies is crucial to developing clear guidelines that address concerns such as fraud, money laundering, and consumer protection without stifling innovation.

User Experience and Education

Cryptocurrency wallets and interfaces can be intimidating for newcomers, presenting a barrier to entry. Improving the user experience through user-friendly interfaces and educational initiatives is vital for widespread adoption. Education campaigns can demystify blockchain technology, explain the benefits of decentralized systems, and guide users on how to securely manage their digital assets. Simplifying the onboarding process will make cryptocurrencies more accessible to a broader audience.

Security Concerns

Security remains a significant challenge in the cryptocurrency space, with high-profile hacks and scams garnering attention. Users need assurance that their digital assets are secure, and the industry must continuously innovate to enhance security measures. Solutions include hardware wallets, secure key management practices, and the implementation of robust security protocols by cryptocurrency exchanges.

Volatility and Price Stability

The price volatility of cryptocurrencies, exemplified by Bitcoin's and other altcoins' price swings, poses challenges for their use in daily transactions and as stores of value. Stablecoins, pegged to traditional fiat currencies, offer a potential solution by providing stability in value while retaining the benefits of blockchain technology. Integrating stablecoins into payment systems and financial applications could mitigate concerns related to cryptocurrency price volatility.

Interoperability and Standardization

The lack of interoperability and standardization among various blockchain networks limits their ability to work seamlessly together. Developing interoperability solutions and industry standards is crucial for facilitating cross-chain transactions and ensuring compatibility between different blockchain platforms. Initiatives like interoperable blockchain protocols and standardized token formats aim to create a more interconnected and user-friendly ecosystem.

Financial Inclusion

Cryptocurrencies have the potential to improve financial inclusion by providing access to financial services for the unbanked and underbanked populations. However, challenges such as limited internet access, lack of infrastructure, and low financial literacy must be addressed. Implementing solutions like mobile-based wallets, offline transactions, and targeted education programs can contribute to greater financial inclusion through cryptocurrency adoption.

Resistance from Traditional Financial Institutions

Traditional financial institutions have been cautious about fully embracing cryptocurrencies due to concerns about competition, regulatory uncertainties, and potential disruptions to their established business models. Bridging the gap between traditional finance and the crypto space requires collaboration and a gradual integration approach. As institutions recognize the benefits of blockchain technology, they may become more open to adopting and incorporating cryptocurrencies into their offerings.

Environmental Concerns

The energy consumption associated with certain consensus mechanisms, particularly Proof of Work (PoW), has raised environmental concerns. Transitioning to more energy-efficient consensus mechanisms, such as Proof of Stake (PoS) or other eco-friendly alternatives, can address these concerns. Additionally, sustainable practices and initiatives within the crypto industry aim to minimize its environmental footprint.

Resistance to Change and Trust Building

Overcoming the inertia and skepticism associated with adopting new financial technologies is a significant challenge. Building trust among users, businesses, and regulators is a continuous process. Transparent communication, industry self-regulation, and showcasing successful use cases can contribute to trust-building efforts and help overcome resistance to change.

Cross-Border Transactions and Financial Inclusion

Cross-border transactions and financial inclusion are intricately linked, and the advent of blockchain technology and cryptocurrencies has the potential to revolutionize both aspects of the global financial system. The synergy between cross-border transactions and financial inclusion in the context of cryptocurrencies has the potential to reshape the global financial landscape. As technology continues to advance and regulatory frameworks evolve, cryptocurrencies may play a pivotal role in creating a more inclusive and efficient financial ecosystem, transcending borders, and empowering individuals worldwide.

Cross-Border Transactions

Traditional cross-border transactions often involve multiple intermediaries, lengthy settlement times, and high fees. The inefficiencies inherent in the current system can be attributed to the use of legacy technologies and complex networks of financial institutions. Blockchain technology, particularly its application in cryptocurrencies, presents a solution to these challenges. Cryptocurrencies, operating on decentralized and immutable blockchains, enable peer-to-peer transactions across borders without the need for intermediaries. This not only reduces transaction costs but also expedites settlement times, providing a faster and more cost-effective alternative to traditional cross-border payment systems.

Financial Inclusion

Financial inclusion, the goal of providing access to affordable and reliable financial services to all individuals, is a global challenge. Many people, especially in developing countries, remain unbanked or underbanked due to factors such as lack of infrastructure, limited access to traditional banking services, and the high costs associated with maintaining bank accounts. Cryptocurrencies, being accessible through digital wallets and not dependent on traditional banking infrastructure, have the potential to bridge this gap. Individuals with access to the internet can participate in the global economy, engage in financial transactions, and store value without relying on traditional banking services.

Remittances

Remittances, or funds sent by individuals working abroad to their home countries, play a significant role in many economies. However, traditional remittance systems are often associated with high fees and extended processing times. Cryptocurrencies offer a more efficient and cost-effective solution for remittances. Blockchain-based platforms enable near-instantaneous cross-border transfers with lower fees, providing a substantial benefit to individuals sending and receiving remittances, particularly in regions where traditional banking infrastructure is limited.

Cryptocurrency as a Cross-Border Solution

Cryptocurrencies such as Bitcoin and stablecoins have emerged as effective tools for facilitating cross-border transactions. Bitcoin, with its decentralized nature and borderless characteristics, allows users to transfer value across borders without the need for intermediaries. Stablecoins pegged to traditional fiat currencies provide a more stable medium of exchange, reducing the volatility associated with some cryptocurrencies. These digital assets open new possibilities for individuals and businesses to engage in cross-border trade and financial activities, fostering economic growth and global interconnectedness.

Overcoming Banking Barriers

Traditional banking systems often pose barriers to financial inclusion, with requirements such as minimum balances, credit checks, and physical presence. Cryptocurrencies remove these barriers by providing an alternative financial infrastructure that operates on a decentralized and permissionless basis. Individuals who lack access to traditional banking services can participate in the digital economy through cryptocurrency transactions, potentially unlocking economic opportunities and fostering greater financial independence.

Empowering the Unbanked

Cryptocurrencies empower the unbanked by offering them a means to store value, send and receive payments, and access a range of financial services directly through their smartphones. This empowerment can lead to increased economic participation, improved savings, and a pathway to breaking the cycle of poverty. Decentralized finance (DeFi) platforms built on blockchain technology further extend financial services, such as lending and borrowing, to individuals who may not have access to traditional banking services.

Regulatory Considerations

For the widespread adoption of cryptocurrencies in cross-border transactions and financial inclusion, regulatory frameworks must evolve to provide clarity and consumer protection. Regulatory bodies worldwide are grappling with the need to strike a balance between fostering innovation and addressing potential risks. A clear regulatory environment can provide the necessary confidence for individuals, businesses, and financial institutions to engage with cryptocurrencies, thereby accelerating their integration into the global financial system.

Challenges and Future Outlook

While the potential benefits are significant, challenges remain. Volatility, regulatory uncertainties, and technological barriers need to be addressed to realize the full potential of cryptocurrencies in cross-border transactions and financial inclusion. Ongoing developments, including central bank digital currencies (CBDCs) and advancements in blockchain technology, are likely to shape the future landscape. Collaborative efforts between the public and private sectors, as well as international cooperation, will be crucial in navigating these challenges and unlocking the transformative potential of cross-border transactions and financial inclusion through cryptocurrencies.

Cryptocurrency in the Everyday Economy

Cryptocurrency's integration into the everyday economy is a transformative trend that holds the potential to redefine traditional financial transactions, payment systems, and the way individuals engage with money daily. The integration of cryptocurrencies into the everyday economy is an ongoing and dynamic process that continues to shape traditional financial paradigms. From daily transactions to new forms of digital ownership, cryptocurrencies are redefining how individuals engage with money, assets, and economic activities. As technological advancements, regulatory clarity, and user awareness progress, the impact of cryptocurrencies on the everyday economy is likely to deepen, contributing to a more decentralized, inclusive, and efficient financial landscape.

Payment Solutions

Cryptocurrencies serve as alternative payment solutions, challenging the conventional methods dominated by credit cards and traditional banking systems. With the rise of platforms and businesses accepting cryptocurrencies, users can make purchases for goods and services using digital assets. This shift represents a departure from traditional payment processes, allowing for faster, borderless transactions that are not subject to the same geographical and bureaucratic limitations as traditional banking systems.

Peer-to-Peer Transactions

Cryptocurrencies facilitate peer-to-peer transactions, enabling individuals to send and receive funds directly without intermediaries. This decentralized nature reduces reliance on traditional banking channels, allowing for quicker and more cost-effective transactions. Peer-to-peer transactions are particularly valuable in cross-border scenarios, where cryptocurrencies offer an efficient and accessible alternative to traditional remittance services.

Decentralized Finance (DeFi)

The emergence of decentralized finance, or DeFi, represents a revolutionary development within the cryptocurrency space. DeFi platforms leverage blockchain technology to recreate traditional financial services such as lending, borrowing, and trading without relying on centralized institutions. This enables individuals to access financial services directly, contributing to financial inclusion by providing alternatives to those who may be excluded from traditional banking systems.

Cryptocurrency Wallets

The adoption of cryptocurrency wallets has become a common feature in the everyday economy. These digital wallets allow users to store, manage, and transact with cryptocurrencies. As technology advances, user-friendly wallet interfaces and mobile applications have made it easier for individuals to navigate the complexities of cryptocurrency ownership and transactions, contributing to a more seamless integration into daily financial activities.

Point-of-Sale Integration

Various businesses and retailers now accept cryptocurrency payments at physical and online points of sale. Cryptocurrency payment processors facilitate the integration of digital assets into traditional payment systems, allowing consumers to use cryptocurrencies for everyday purchases. This integration reflects a growing acceptance of cryptocurrencies as a legitimate and practical means of exchange in daily economic transactions.

Tokenization of Assets

The tokenization of real-world assets, such as real estate, art, and commodities, further extends the impact of cryptocurrencies in the everyday economy. By representing these assets as digital tokens on blockchain networks, individuals gain access to fractional ownership, liquidity, and the ability to trade traditionally illiquid assets. This innovation broadens investment opportunities and democratizes access to a diverse range of assets.

Micropayments and Microtransactions

Cryptocurrencies are particularly well-suited for micropayments and microtransactions due to their divisibility and low transaction costs. This has implications for content creators, online platforms, and service providers where small, frequent transactions are common. Cryptocurrencies enable efficient and instantaneous payments for digital content, services, and other online activities, fostering new economic models and revenue streams.

Employment and Freelancing

The gig economy and freelance work have witnessed the integration of cryptocurrencies for payments. Freelancers and remote workers can receive payments in cryptocurrencies, providing a borderless and efficient means of compensation. This is especially advantageous for individuals working across international borders, eliminating the need for currency conversions and reducing transaction costs associated with traditional payment methods.

NFTs and Digital Ownership

The rise of non-fungible tokens (NFTs) has introduced a new dimension to the everyday economy, emphasizing digital ownership and authenticity. NFTs, representing unique digital or physical assets on blockchain, allow individuals to buy, sell, and trade digital art, collectibles, and other digital assets securely. This trend demonstrates the transformative potential of cryptocurrencies in redefining concepts of ownership and value in the digital age.

Regulatory Considerations and Consumer Protection

As cryptocurrencies become more integrated into the everyday economy, regulatory frameworks are evolving to address consumer protection and ensure the responsible use of digital assets. Governments and regulatory bodies are working to establish guidelines that balance innovation with safeguarding user interests, fostering a regulatory environment that can enhance trust and confidence in cryptocurrency adoption.

VIII. Security and Privacy Challenges

Addressing Security Concerns in Cryptocurrency

Addressing security concerns in cryptocurrency is a critical aspect of ensuring the trust and adoption of digital assets in the global financial landscape. As the cryptocurrency space evolves, various measures and innovations are being implemented to enhance the security of blockchain networks, cryptocurrency exchanges, and individual user holdings.

Addressing security concerns in cryptocurrency is an ongoing and collaborative effort that involves technological advancements, regulatory compliance, and user education. As the industry matures, the implementation of robust security measures at various levels, from blockchain protocols to individual user practices, is essential to build and maintain trust in the cryptocurrency ecosystem. By fostering a security-first mindset and embracing innovative solutions, the cryptocurrency community can mitigate risks and create a more secure foundation for the future of digital finance.

Blockchain Security

Blockchain, the underlying technology of most cryptocurrencies, relies on cryptographic principles to secure transactions and maintain the integrity of the decentralized ledger. The immutability and transparency of blockchain contribute to its robust security. The consensus mechanisms, such as Proof of Work (PoW) and Proof of Stake (PoS), play a crucial role in preventing fraudulent activities and ensuring the validity of transactions. Ongoing research and development in cryptographic techniques continue to strengthen the security foundations of blockchain networks.

Cryptographic Techniques

Cryptography is fundamental to the security of cryptocurrencies. Public-key cryptography, where users have a public key for receiving funds and a private key for authorizing transactions, forms the basis of secure cryptocurrency transactions. Advanced cryptographic techniques, including zero-knowledge proofs and homomorphic encryption, are explored to enhance privacy and security within blockchain networks. As the field of cryptography evolves, the industry adapts to integrate cutting-edge solutions to address emerging security challenges.

Secure Wallets

Cryptocurrency wallets are essential tools for users to store and manage their digital assets. Securing these wallets is paramount to preventing unauthorized access and potential loss of funds. Hardware wallets, which store private keys offline, offer enhanced security compared to software wallets that may be vulnerable to online threats. Users are encouraged to choose reputable wallet providers, employ strong passwords, and implement additional security features such as two-factor authentication (2FA) to safeguard their cryptocurrency holdings.

Exchange Security

Cryptocurrency exchanges, where users trade and convert digital assets, are frequent targets for cyberattacks. High-profile exchange hacks have underscored the need for robust security measures. Exchange platforms are implementing multi-layered security protocols, including cold storage of funds, regular security audits, and advanced encryption techniques to protect user accounts and assets. Regulatory compliance and adherence to industry best practices further contribute to the overall security posture of cryptocurrency exchanges.

Two-Factor Authentication (2FA)

Two-factor authentication is a widely adopted security measure that adds an additional layer of protection to user accounts. By requiring users to provide a second form of verification, typically through a mobile app or SMS, 2FA mitigates the risk of unauthorized access even if login credentials are compromised. Users are strongly encouraged to enable 2FA on their cryptocurrency exchange accounts and wallets to enhance security.

Regulatory Compliance

Regulatory frameworks play a crucial role in addressing security concerns in the cryptocurrency space. Governments and regulatory bodies are working to establish clear guidelines for cryptocurrency exchanges and service providers. Compliance with Know Your Customer (KYC) and Anti-Money Laundering (AML) regulations helps prevent illicit activities and enhances the overall security of the cryptocurrency ecosystem.

Smart Contract Audits

Smart contracts, self-executing contracts with the terms of the agreement directly written into code, are a key feature of many blockchain platforms. Ensuring the security of smart contracts is vital to prevent vulnerabilities that could be exploited by malicious actors. Smart contract audits, conducted by specialized firms, help identify and address potential security flaws in the code before deployment, reducing the risk of contract-related vulnerabilities.

Education and User Awareness

Promoting education and awareness among cryptocurrency users is a proactive approach to addressing security concerns. Users need to understand the potential risks, employ best practices for securing their assets, and stay informed about the evolving threat landscape.

Educational initiatives, community forums, and outreach efforts contribute to a more informed and security-conscious user base.

Bug Bounty Programs

Cryptocurrency projects and exchanges often implement bug bounty programs, inviting security researchers and ethical hackers to identify and report vulnerabilities. These programs incentivize the discovery and responsible disclosure of security issues, allowing development teams to promptly address potential threats before they can be exploited maliciously.

Continuous Improvement and Collaboration

The dynamic nature of the cybersecurity landscape requires continuous improvement and collaboration within the cryptocurrency community. Industry stakeholders, including developers, exchanges, regulators, and users, must work together to share insights, address emerging threats, and implement effective security measures. Collaborative efforts contribute to a more resilient and secure cryptocurrency ecosystem.

Privacy Coins and Anonymity

Privacy coins represent a distinct category within the cryptocurrency space, offering enhanced anonymity and privacy features compared to traditional cryptocurrencies like Bitcoin. These digital assets prioritize the confidentiality of transactions, addressing concerns about financial privacy and surveillance. Privacy coins employ various cryptographic techniques to obfuscate transaction details and protect user identities, fostering a greater degree of anonymity in financial transactions.

Privacy coins play a crucial role in addressing concerns about financial privacy and transactional surveillance within the cryptocurrency ecosystem. By employing advanced cryptographic techniques, these coins provide users with enhanced anonymity, contributing to a more private and decentralized financial landscape. However, the evolving regulatory landscape and ethical considerations highlight the need for a thoughtful and collaborative approach to ensure the responsible use of privacy coins in the broader context of digital finance.

Cryptographic Privacy Techniques

Privacy coins leverage advanced cryptographic techniques to enhance privacy. Ring signatures, implemented by cryptocurrencies like Monero, mix a user's transaction with those of others, making it challenging to trace the origin of funds. Zero-knowledge proofs, such as zk-SNARKs (Zero-Knowledge Succinct Non-Interactive Arguments of Knowledge), enable the verification of transaction validity without revealing specific details, enhancing transaction privacy. These cryptographic methods are instrumental in achieving a higher level of anonymity compared to transparent blockchain transactions.

Transactional Privacy

Privacy coins prioritize transactional privacy by concealing the sender, receiver, and transaction amount. In contrast to transparent blockchains, where transaction details are publicly visible, privacy coins obscure this information. This focus on transactional privacy addresses concerns about the surveillance of financial activities, offering users a greater degree of confidentiality in their digital transactions.

User Identity Protection

Privacy coins aim to protect user identities by minimizing the traceability of transactions. Anonymity features, such as stealth addresses and one-time addresses, ensure that the recipient's identity remains confidential. Stealth addresses generate unique addresses for each transaction, making it difficult to link multiple transactions to a single user. These privacy-enhancing features contribute to a more robust shield against the identification of users participating in the cryptocurrency ecosystem.

Decentralization and Trustlessness

Privacy coins align with the core principles of decentralization and trust lessness inherent in cryptocurrency. By prioritizing user privacy, these coins reduce dependence on centralized authorities and intermediaries. Users can transact directly with each other without relying on third parties, fostering a peer-to-peer network where financial interactions are decentralized, and trust is established through cryptographic consensus mechanisms.

Monero: A Pioneer in Privacy

Monero stands out as a pioneer among privacy coins, prioritizing user privacy and fungibility. Monero utilizes a combination of ring signatures, stealth addresses, and confidential transactions to provide a high level of transactional privacy. Fungibility ensures that each unit of Monero is indistinguishable from another, preventing discrimination based on transaction history. This commitment to privacy has positioned Monero as a leading choice for users seeking enhanced anonymity in their cryptocurrency transactions.

Zcash: Privacy with Optional Transparency

Zcash takes a unique approach to privacy by offering users the option of shielded or transparent transactions. Shielded transactions utilize zk-SNARKs to provide enhanced privacy, while transparent transactions function similarly to traditional blockchain transactions. This dual approach allows users to choose the level of privacy they desire, making Zcash a versatile privacy coin within the cryptocurrency landscape.

Regulatory Considerations

The privacy features of these coins have attracted attention from regulators and law enforcement agencies concerned about the potential misuse of anonymity in financial transactions. While privacy coins aim to protect user privacy, they also face challenges related to regulatory compliance. Striking a balance between privacy and regulatory requirements remains a complex and evolving aspect of the privacy coin ecosystem.

Evolving Technologies

The field of privacy coins continues to evolve, with ongoing research and development focused on enhancing privacy features and mitigating potential vulnerabilities. Innovations such as Bulletproofs, which reduce transaction size and improve efficiency, demonstrate the commitment of privacy coin projects to advancing their technologies while maintaining a strong emphasis on user privacy.

Privacy Coins and Financial Inclusion

Privacy coins can contribute to financial inclusion by providing individuals with enhanced privacy protections. In regions where financial surveillance is prevalent or where individuals seek to protect their financial privacy, privacy coins offer a viable solution. The ability to transact privately empowers users who may otherwise be excluded or monitored within traditional financial systems.

Ethical Considerations

The use of privacy coins raises ethical considerations, as the enhanced anonymity they provide can be utilized for both legitimate and potentially illicit purposes. Striking a balance between privacy rights and the prevention of illicit activities remains a nuanced challenge, requiring ongoing dialogue between the cryptocurrency community, regulators, and stakeholders.

Legal and Ethical Implications of Privacy in Cryptocurrency

The legal and ethical implications of privacy in cryptocurrency form a complex and evolving landscape, reflecting the tension between individual privacy rights, regulatory imperatives, and societal expectations. As privacy-focused cryptocurrencies gain popularity, concerns and debates arise regarding their compliance with existing legal frameworks, potential misuse in illicit activities, and the broader ethical considerations surrounding financial privacy.

These implications of privacy in cryptocurrency are multifaceted, requiring a nuanced approach that considers individual rights, regulatory requirements, and the broader societal impact of financial privacy. As the cryptocurrency space continues to evolve, ongoing dialogue and collaboration will be essential to strike a balance that preserves user privacy while addressing legitimate concerns about illicit activities and regulatory compliance.

Privacy Rights vs. Regulatory Compliance

Cryptocurrencies designed for enhanced privacy, such as Monero and Zcash, often clash with regulatory requirements that mandate transparent financial transactions. The tension between user privacy rights and regulatory compliance is a central theme in the legal discourse surrounding privacy coins. While individuals seek greater confidentiality in financial transactions, regulators aim to prevent money laundering, fraud, and illicit activities, necessitating a delicate balance between privacy and adherence to legal standards.

Anti-Money Laundering (AML) and Know Your Customer (KYC) Compliance

Cryptocurrency exchanges and service providers are subject to AML and KYC regulations to prevent illicit financial activities. Privacy coins, by design, can complicate compliance efforts, as the enhanced anonymity they offer may run afoul of AML requirements. Striking a balance that preserves user privacy while ensuring compliance with regulatory standards remains a challenge for both privacy coin projects and regulatory authorities.

Regulatory Scrutiny and Enforcement

Privacy coins have faced increasing regulatory scrutiny, with authorities expressing concerns about the potential misuse of these assets in illicit activities such as money laundering and terrorist financing. Governments and regulatory bodies worldwide are working to establish clear guidelines to address these concerns, leading to an evolving regulatory landscape for privacy-focused cryptocurrencies.

Ethical Considerations of Financial Privacy

The ethical considerations surrounding financial privacy in cryptocurrency extend beyond legal compliance. Advocates argue that financial privacy is a fundamental human right, allowing individuals to maintain autonomy over their economic activities. In this view, privacy coins are seen as tools that empower individuals by providing a layer of confidentiality in their financial transactions, shielding them from unwarranted surveillance and potential discrimination based on financial history.

Prevention of Illicit Activities

While privacy coins offer enhanced confidentiality, concerns persist about their potential use in facilitating illicit activities, including money laundering, tax evasion, and the financing of criminal enterprises. Striking a balance between privacy and preventing illegal actions poses ethical challenges, and ongoing efforts within the cryptocurrency community aim to address these concerns through collaboration with regulators and law enforcement.

De-Anonymization Efforts

In response to regulatory concerns and efforts to prevent illicit activities, some privacy coins have faced attempts at de-anonymization. Researchers and law enforcement agencies explore methods to trace transactions and identify users within privacy-focused blockchain networks. This ongoing cat-and-mouse game between privacy coin developers and de-anonymization efforts raises ethical questions about the limits of surveillance and the preservation of individual privacy.

Trust and Transparency

Trust is a crucial component of the cryptocurrency ecosystem, and privacy coins navigate a delicate balance between providing privacy and maintaining transparency. Transparent blockchain transactions, as seen in Bitcoin, provide a publicly auditable ledger, contributing to trust in the system. Privacy coins must address concerns about trust and transparency while upholding their commitment to user privacy, requiring transparent communication and community engagement.

Financial Inclusion and Privacy

Privacy in cryptocurrency also intersects with the ethical consideration of financial inclusion. In regions where financial surveillance is pervasive, privacy coins may empower individuals who seek to protect their financial privacy and engage in economic activities without fear of censorship or discrimination. This ethical dimension emphasizes the potential positive impact of privacy-focused cryptocurrencies on broader financial inclusion efforts.

Evolving Legal Frameworks

As the cryptocurrency landscape matures, legal frameworks are evolving to accommodate the unique features of privacy coins. Some jurisdictions are developing specific regulations that recognize the nuances of privacy-focused cryptocurrencies, aiming to provide clarity for both users and service providers. The challenge lies in crafting regulations that address legitimate privacy concerns while preventing misuse.

Collaboration and Dialogue

Addressing the legal and ethical implications of privacy in cryptocurrency requires collaboration between stakeholders, including privacy coin developers, regulators, law enforcement agencies, and the broader cryptocurrency community. Open dialogue and cooperation are essential to navigating the complex intersection of privacy, regulation, and ethics, ensuring that legal frameworks and ethical considerations align to foster a responsible and inclusive cryptocurrency ecosystem.

IX. Social and Environmental Impact

Cryptocurrency and Social Change

Cryptocurrency's impact on social change is a multifaceted and dynamic phenomenon, influencing various aspects of society, finance, and individual empowerment. From financial inclusion to decentralized governance models, cryptocurrencies have the potential to reshape traditional power structures and foster positive social transformation. Cryptocurrency's impact on social change is multifaceted, spanning financial inclusion, empowerment, decentralized governance, and philanthropy. As the crypto space continues to evolve, it is crucial to navigate the challenges and ethical considerations to maximize the positive contributions of cryptocurrencies to societal transformation.

Financial Inclusion

One of the most significant contributions of cryptocurrency to social change is in the realm of financial inclusion. Cryptocurrencies provide an alternative financial infrastructure that operates outside traditional banking systems, offering individuals without access to banking services an opportunity to participate in the global economy. With just a smartphone and internet access, people in underserved regions can engage in financial transactions, access savings, and explore new economic opportunities, thereby breaking down barriers to financial inclusion.

Empowering the Unbanked

Cryptocurrencies empower the unbanked by giving them control over their finances without the need for traditional banking services. Individuals who lack access to banking infrastructure can use cryptocurrencies for payments, savings, and investments. This empowerment has the potential to uplift communities by providing a means of financial independence and reducing dependence on centralized financial institutions.

Remittances and Cross-Border Transactions

Cryptocurrencies facilitate efficient and cost-effective cross-border transactions, especially for remittances. Traditional remittance services are often associated with high fees and delays. Cryptocurrencies offer a faster and more affordable alternative, enabling individuals to send and receive funds across borders without the need for intermediaries. This has a direct impact on the livelihoods of individuals relying on remittances, contributing to economic stability and poverty reduction.

Decentralized Governance Models

Cryptocurrencies and blockchain technology introduce decentralized governance models that challenge traditional hierarchical structures. Decentralized Autonomous Organizations (DAOs) exemplify this shift by allowing community members to participate in decision-making processes without reliance on central authorities. This innovative governance model has the potential to foster more inclusive and transparent decision-making in various sectors, from finance to social organizations.

Community Empowerment

Cryptocurrencies often emerge from and are sustained by vibrant and engaged communities. These communities foster collaboration, information-sharing, and collective problem-solving. Through token-based ecosystems, users are incentivized to contribute to the growth and development of projects, creating a sense of ownership and empowerment. This community-driven ethos has the potential to extend beyond the crypto space, influencing collaborative efforts in other areas of society.

Funding Mechanisms for Social Causes

Cryptocurrencies enable novel funding mechanisms for social causes through Initial Coin Offerings (ICOs) and token sales. Projects with a social impact focus can raise funds directly from a global audience, bypassing traditional fundraising channels. This democratization of funding allows for a broader range of initiatives addressing social challenges to secure financial support, fostering innovation and creativity in the pursuit of positive social change.

Privacy and Autonomy

Cryptocurrencies, particularly privacy-focused ones, provide users with greater control over their financial privacy. Individuals can conduct transactions without revealing personal information, offering a level of anonymity not typically available in traditional financial systems. This emphasis on privacy aligns with the broader movement advocating for individual autonomy and protection from unwarranted surveillance.

Philanthropy and Charitable Contributions

Cryptocurrencies have facilitated philanthropy and charitable contributions through blockchain-based donation platforms. These platforms leverage the transparency and traceability of blockchain to ensure that donated funds are used for their intended purposes. Cryptocurrencies enable seamless, borderless donations, allowing individuals from around the world to contribute to social causes, disaster relief, and charitable projects.

Democratizing Access to Investments

Through tokenization, cryptocurrencies democratize access to investment opportunities, allowing a broader range of individuals to participate in traditionally exclusive markets such as real estate, art, and startups. This democratization of investment opportunities has the potential to redistribute wealth and foster a more inclusive economic landscape.

Challenges and Ethical Considerations

While cryptocurrencies offer significant potential for social change, challenges and ethical considerations persist. Issues such as regulatory uncertainty, market volatility, and the potential for misuse in illicit activities necessitate careful consideration. Striking a balance between innovation, regulatory compliance, and ethical use is essential to harness the positive potential of cryptocurrencies for social change.

Environmental Concerns and Solutions

The environmental concerns associated with cryptocurrency, particularly Bitcoin, have become a focal point of discussion as the popularity and energy consumption of blockchain networks continue to rise. While the decentralized and secure nature of blockchain technology is celebrated, the environmental impact, particularly in terms of energy consumption and electronic waste, has raised valid concerns.

Addressing the environmental concerns associated with cryptocurrency requires a multifaceted approach that includes the adoption of renewable energy, the transition to energy-efficient consensus mechanisms, community-driven initiatives, and regulatory considerations. Striking a balance between the transformative potential of blockchain technology and environmental sustainability is essential to ensure the long-term viability and responsible growth of the cryptocurrency industry.

Energy Consumption

One of the primary environmental concerns in cryptocurrency is the significant energy consumption associated with mining activities, particularly in the case of Proof of Work (PoW) consensus algorithms. Bitcoin, the largest and most well-known cryptocurrency, relies on PoW, where miners compete to solve complex mathematical problems to validate transactions and secure the network. This process demands an enormous amount of computational power, leading to a substantial carbon footprint and energy consumption. Critics argue that the energy-intensive nature of PoW cryptocurrencies contributes to climate change and contradicts global efforts to reduce carbon emissions.

Electronic Waste

The electronic waste generated by obsolete mining hardware and cryptocurrency-related equipment is another environmental challenge. As newer, more efficient mining hardware is developed, older devices become obsolete and are often discarded. This electronic waste, which may contain hazardous materials, contributes to environmental pollution if not properly managed. Sustainable disposal and recycling practices are crucial to mitigate the environmental impact of electronic waste generated by the cryptocurrency industry.

Renewable Energy Adoption

A potential solution to the environmental impact of cryptocurrency is the increased adoption of renewable energy sources for mining operations. Some mining facilities and projects are actively seeking to use renewable energy, such as solar or wind power, to address concerns about carbon emissions. The transition to sustainable energy practices could significantly reduce the overall environmental footprint of cryptocurrencies and align them with global efforts to combat climate change.

Transition to Proof of Stake (PoS)

To address the energy consumption concerns associated with PoW consensus algorithms, there is a growing movement toward adopting Proof of Stake (PoS) and other energy-efficient consensus mechanisms. PoS relies on validators who hold a stake in the cryptocurrency to create new blocks and validate transactions. Unlike PoW, PoS does not require the intense computational work associated with mining, making it a more energy-efficient alternative. Ethereum, the second-largest cryptocurrency by market capitalization, is in the process of transitioning from PoW to PoS.

Layer 2 Scaling Solutions

Layer 2 scaling solutions, such as the Lightning Network for Bitcoin and the various scaling solutions for Ethereum, aim to reduce the load on the main blockchain by enabling faster and more cost-effective transactions. By processing a large number of transactions off-chain and settling them on the main blockchain only when necessary, these solutions aim to improve scalability and reduce the energy consumption associated with each transaction.

Carbon Offsetting Initiatives

Some cryptocurrency projects and organizations are exploring carbon offsetting initiatives as a way to neutralize the environmental impact of their operations. Carbon offsetting involves investing in projects that reduce or capture an equivalent amount of greenhouse gases to balance out the emissions generated. While not a direct solution to the energy consumption of mining, carbon offsetting initiatives are seen as a step toward environmental responsibility within the cryptocurrency industry.

Community-Led Sustainability Initiatives

The cryptocurrency community itself plays a role in addressing environmental concerns. There is a growing awareness and advocacy for sustainable practices within the community, urging projects and stakeholders to consider the environmental impact of their activities. Community-led initiatives focus on promoting transparency, accountability, and responsible environmental practices, driving positive change from within the cryptocurrency ecosystem.

Education and Awareness

Educating the cryptocurrency community and the general public about the environmental impact of blockchain technology is crucial for fostering responsible practices. Increased awareness can drive demand for environmentally friendly solutions, influence industry standards, and encourage the adoption of sustainable technologies. Education initiatives can also highlight the potential of blockchain technology to contribute positively to environmental causes, such as transparent supply chains and carbon offset tracking.

Regulatory Considerations

Governments and regulatory bodies are starting to address the environmental impact of cryptocurrency through regulations and standards. Some jurisdictions are exploring policies that incentivize the use of renewable energy in mining operations or impose restrictions on energy-intensive cryptocurrencies. Regulatory frameworks that encourage environmentally friendly practices can play a significant role in shaping the industry's environmental impact.

Technological Innovations

Ongoing technological innovations within the cryptocurrency space aim to reduce the environmental impact of blockchain networks. Research and development efforts focus on creating more energy-efficient consensus mechanisms, improving scalability, and exploring novel approaches to minimize the carbon footprint. These innovations, coupled with a commitment to sustainability, have the potential to reshape the environmental narrative surrounding cryptocurrencies.

Cryptocurrency Philanthropy and Community Development

Cryptocurrency philanthropy and community development represent a powerful intersection where innovative financial technologies meet social impact. As the crypto space continues to mature, an increasing number of projects and individuals are leveraging digital assets to drive positive change, fostering community development, and contributing to charitable causes.

Cryptocurrency philanthropy and community development represent a dynamic and evolving landscape within the broader crypto ecosystem. By leveraging the unique features of blockchain technology, including transparency, decentralization, and borderless transactions, the crypto community has the potential to drive positive social change. Whether through decentralized fundraising, community-led initiatives, or impact investing, cryptocurrency philanthropy showcases the transformative power of digital assets in addressing global challenges and fostering community development.

Decentralized Fundraising

Cryptocurrency has revolutionized fundraising by providing a decentralized and borderless mechanism for collecting donations. Through Initial Coin Offerings (ICOs) or token sales, projects can raise funds directly from a global audience, bypassing traditional fundraising channels. This democratization of fundraising allows for more inclusive participation and enables projects with social impact goals to access a diverse pool of supporters.

Charitable Cryptocurrency Foundations

Several cryptocurrency projects and organizations have established foundations dedicated to philanthropy and community development. These foundations allocate a portion of their resources or token holdings to support charitable initiatives and projects that align with their mission. The Ethereum Foundation, for example, has a history of supporting projects focused on education, research, and community development within the Ethereum ecosystem.

Blockchain for Social Impact

The concept of "Blockchain for Social Impact" has gained momentum, emphasizing the use of blockchain technology to address global challenges and promote positive social change. Initiatives within this realm explore applications of blockchain, such as transparent supply chains, identity verification for refugees, and tracking charitable donations to ensure they reach their intended recipients. These projects showcase the potential of blockchain technology beyond financial transactions.

Community-Led Initiatives

Cryptocurrency communities themselves often spearhead philanthropic initiatives. Community-led efforts involve rallying support for charitable causes, fundraising campaigns, or community development projects. These initiatives showcase the altruistic nature of the crypto community, emphasizing a sense of shared responsibility and the belief in using technology for the greater good.

Cryptocurrency Donations to NGOs

Non-governmental organizations (NGOs) are increasingly accepting cryptocurrency donations as a means to diversify their funding sources. Cryptocurrency donations provide a transparent and traceable way to track funds, reducing the risk of mismanagement or corruption. The Pineapple Fund, an anonymous donor who distributed a significant amount of Bitcoin to various charitable causes, exemplifies the transformative potential of crypto philanthropy.

Financial Inclusion and Empowerment

Cryptocurrency plays a role in financial inclusion and empowerment, particularly in regions with limited access to traditional banking services. By providing individuals with the ability to send and receive funds globally, cryptocurrencies empower communities to participate in the global economy, fostering economic development and reducing financial exclusion.

Impact Investing through Tokens

The rise of impact investing through tokens allows investors to support projects that align with their values. Socially responsible tokens, often issued by projects with a philanthropic focus, provide a mechanism for investors to contribute to causes they believe in while potentially benefiting from the project's success. This approach blends financial returns with social impact, creating a new paradigm for responsible investing.

Education and Skill Development

Philanthropic efforts in the cryptocurrency space extend beyond monetary donations to include education and skill development initiatives. Projects allocate resources to educate communities about blockchain technology, cryptocurrency, and the broader implications of decentralized systems. By fostering understanding and skill development, these initiatives contribute to building a more knowledgeable and empowered global community.

Disaster Relief and Humanitarian Aid

Cryptocurrencies offer a rapid and transparent way to provide disaster relief and humanitarian aid. During crises, decentralized donations can quickly reach affected regions, bypassing traditional financial systems and minimizing delays. This agility and transparency enhance the efficiency and impact of charitable efforts in times of need.

Transparent Donation Tracking

Blockchain's transparency allows donors to track their contributions in real-time, ensuring that funds are utilized as intended. This level of transparency builds trust between donors and charitable organizations, addressing concerns related to accountability and mismanagement. Transparent donation tracking enhances the credibility of philanthropic initiatives within the crypto space.

X. The Role of Governments and Regulation

National and International Regulatory Frameworks

The regulatory frameworks governing cryptocurrency are complex and rapidly evolving on both national and international levels. Governments and regulatory bodies around the world are grappling with the challenges posed by the decentralized nature of cryptocurrencies, aiming to strike a balance between fostering innovation and protecting investors, consumers, and the financial system.

The regulatory landscape for cryptocurrencies is a dynamic and evolving domain shaped by the interplay of national and international efforts. Clear definitions, licensing requirements, consumer protection measures, and international coordination are essential components of effective regulatory frameworks. As the cryptocurrency space continues to mature, regulatory initiatives will likely intensify, requiring ongoing collaboration and adaptation to ensure the responsible growth of this transformative sector.

National Regulatory Frameworks

Countries adopt varied approaches to regulate cryptocurrencies, reflecting diverse attitudes toward digital assets. Some nations embrace and provide a conducive environment for cryptocurrency innovation, implementing clear regulations to foster industry growth. Others approach the sector cautiously, implementing measures to mitigate risks associated with fraud, money laundering, and consumer protection.

Clear Definitions and Classification

National regulatory frameworks often begin with clear definitions and classifications of cryptocurrencies and related activities. Distinguishing between different types of tokens, such as utility tokens and security tokens, helps regulators tailor specific rules for each category. Clear definitions contribute to legal certainty and enable businesses to navigate the regulatory landscape more effectively.

Licensing and Registration

Many countries require cryptocurrency exchanges and wallet providers to obtain licenses or register with regulatory authorities. These measures aim to ensure that these entities adhere to specific standards, such as anti-money laundering (AML) and know your customer (KYC) procedures. Licensing and registration provide a level of oversight and accountability, reducing the risk of illicit activities within the cryptocurrency ecosystem.

Consumer Protection

Regulators often focus on consumer protection measures to safeguard investors and users of cryptocurrency services. This includes implementing disclosure requirements, ensuring transparent communication of risks, and addressing issues related to fraud and market manipulation. Regulatory bodies may also establish mechanisms for handling consumer complaints and disputes within the cryptocurrency sector.

Taxation and Reporting

Taxation of cryptocurrency transactions is a crucial aspect of regulatory frameworks. Many countries have introduced tax guidelines for individuals and businesses engaged in cryptocurrency activities. Reporting requirements aim to track transactions and holdings for taxation purposes, contributing to the broader goal of ensuring compliance with existing tax laws.

Anti-Money Laundering (AML) and Combating the Financing of Terrorism (CFT)

Addressing concerns related to money laundering and the financing of terrorism is a top priority for regulators. Cryptocurrency exchanges and service providers are often required to implement robust AML and CFT measures, including customer due diligence and suspicious transaction reporting. These efforts align with international standards set by organizations like the Financial Action Task Force (FATF).

International Regulatory Frameworks

Given the global nature of cryptocurrencies, there is a growing need for international coordination in regulatory efforts. Cross-border transactions and the borderless nature of blockchain technology make it challenging for individual countries to regulate the space effectively in isolation.

Financial Action Task Force (FATF)

The FATF plays a central role in shaping international standards for combating money laundering and terrorist financing. In recent years, the FATF has extended its guidance to include recommendations specific to the regulation of virtual assets and virtual asset service providers. Member countries are expected to align their national regulatory frameworks with these recommendations.

Coordination through International Organizations

International organizations, such as the International Monetary Fund (IMF) and the World Bank, contribute to discussions on the global regulatory landscape for cryptocurrencies. These organizations facilitate information exchange and coordination among member countries, aiming to address challenges related to financial stability, consumer protection, and the prevention of illicit activities.

G20 Initiatives

The Group of Twenty (G20) has recognized the need for coordinated efforts in regulating cryptocurrencies. G20 summits have featured discussions on the challenges and opportunities presented by digital assets. While member countries may adopt diverse approaches at the national level, these discussions contribute to a shared understanding of the global implications of cryptocurrency regulation.

European Union (EU) Framework

The European Union has been proactive in developing a comprehensive regulatory framework for cryptocurrencies. The Markets in Crypto Assets (MiCA) proposal, part of the broader Digital Finance Package, aims to establish a harmonized regulatory framework for crypto assets across EU member states. The proposal includes provisions for licensing, investor protection, and market integrity.

Challenges and Future Directions

Despite progress, challenges persist in developing effective national and international regulatory frameworks for cryptocurrencies. The dynamic nature of the industry, technological advancements, and the need for ongoing adaptation to emerging risks make regulatory efforts a continuous process. Striking the right balance between fostering innovation and protecting stakeholders remains a complex task for regulators worldwide.

Government Adoption of Cryptocurrency

The adoption of cryptocurrency by governments represents a transformative shift in the traditional financial landscape. While the cryptocurrency space was initially conceived as a decentralized alternative to government-backed currencies, governments worldwide are increasingly exploring ways to integrate digital assets into their financial systems. This adoption is driven by a recognition of the potential benefits offered by cryptocurrencies, such as increased financial inclusivity, efficiency gains, and the embrace of blockchain technology.

The government adoption of cryptocurrency is a multifaceted phenomenon reflecting a shift in the global financial landscape. From the exploration of CBDCs to the embrace of blockchain technology, governments are navigating the opportunities and challenges presented by digital assets. The coming years are likely to witness further evolution in government approaches to cryptocurrency, as policymakers seek to harness the benefits while mitigating potential risks in this rapidly evolving space.

Central Bank Digital Currencies (CBDCs)

A notable avenue of government adoption is the exploration and development of Central Bank Digital Currencies (CBDCs). CBDCs are digital representations of a country's national currency issued by its central bank. Government's view CBDCs as a means to modernize payment systems, enhance financial inclusion, and improve the efficiency of cross-border transactions. Countries like China have taken significant strides in piloting and implementing CBDCs, marking a shift toward the digitization of sovereign currencies.

Regulatory Clarity and Compliance

Governments recognize the importance of providing regulatory clarity to the burgeoning cryptocurrency industry. Establishing clear regulations fosters a more stable and secure environment for both businesses and consumers. Regulatory frameworks typically address issues such as anti-money laundering (AML) measures, know your customer (KYC) requirements, and tax obligations. Countries like

Switzerland, Singapore, and the United States have made strides in creating comprehensive regulatory frameworks that balance innovation with consumer protection.

Blockchain Technology Adoption

Beyond cryptocurrency itself, governments are increasingly adopting blockchain technology, the underlying technology behind many cryptocurrencies. Blockchain offers transparency, security, and efficiency in record-keeping, making it attractive for various government applications. Governments explore the use of blockchain in areas such as supply chain management, identity verification, voting systems, and property registries to enhance transparency and reduce fraud.

Sovereign Wealth Funds and Investments

Some governments are considering the inclusion of cryptocurrencies, particularly Bitcoin, in their sovereign wealth funds. The idea is to diversify investment portfolios and potentially benefit from the potential growth of digital assets. While this approach is not universal, it underscores a growing acknowledgment of the legitimacy and potential value of cryptocurrencies as financial instruments.

Fostering Innovation and Startups

Governments recognize the role of cryptocurrencies in fostering innovation and supporting the growth of startups in the financial technology (FinTech) sector. By providing a supportive regulatory environment and, in some cases, financial incentives, governments aim to position themselves as hubs for cryptocurrency and blockchain innovation. Countries like Estonia and Malta have actively embraced this approach, attracting cryptocurrency businesses and startups to establish operations within their borders.

Economic Competitiveness

Governments are mindful of the potential economic advantages associated with the adoption of cryptocurrencies. By embracing digital currencies and blockchain technology, countries seek to enhance their competitiveness in the global economy. This includes positioning themselves as leaders in financial innovation, attracting investment, and developing a skilled workforce in blockchain-related fields.

Cross-Border Payments and Trade

Cryptocurrencies offer the potential for more efficient and cost-effective cross-border payments and trade. Governments, recognizing the limitations of traditional banking systems in this regard, are exploring how cryptocurrencies can streamline international transactions. The use of stablecoins pegged to national currencies is one avenue being explored to facilitate faster and more affordable cross-border payments.

Financial Inclusion and Digital Wallets

In regions where traditional banking infrastructure is limited, governments are turning to cryptocurrencies to promote financial inclusion. By introducing digital wallets and encouraging the use of cryptocurrencies, especially in areas with a large unbanked population, governments aim to provide citizens with access to financial services and empower them economically.

Cybersecurity and National Security Considerations

Governments are increasingly cognizant of the cybersecurity and national security implications associated with cryptocurrencies. While recognizing the potential benefits, governments are also focused on addressing concerns related to illicit activities, fraud, and the potential use of digital assets for illegal purposes. Striking a balance between innovation and security remains a key challenge in the government adoption of cryptocurrencies.

Public Awareness and Education

To facilitate widespread adoption and acceptance, governments are investing in public awareness and education campaigns about cryptocurrencies. By promoting a better understanding of digital assets and blockchain technology, governments aim to alleviate concerns, build trust, and encourage responsible use of cryptocurrencies among their citizens.

Balancing Innovation and Regulation

Balancing innovation and regulation are a delicate dance, particularly in industries that undergo rapid technological advancements, such as the cryptocurrency and blockchain sector. The tension between fostering innovation and ensuring consumer protection, financial stability, and regulatory compliance poses a significant challenge for policymakers and regulators worldwide.

Finding the right balance between innovation and regulation in the cryptocurrency and blockchain space is an ongoing challenge. Governments are navigating uncharted territories, aiming to foster innovation while safeguarding the interests of consumers and maintaining financial stability. A collaborative, iterative, and adaptive regulatory approach, coupled with industry engagement and ethical considerations, is essential to successfully navigate this complex and rapidly evolving landscape. Striking this balance is crucial to unlocking the full potential of transformative technologies while mitigating potential risks.

Promoting Innovation

Innovation is the lifeblood of progress, and in the realm of cryptocurrency and blockchain technology, it drives transformative change. Governments recognize the potential benefits of fostering innovation in this space, including increased financial inclusion, enhanced efficiency in financial transactions, and the development of novel solutions to age-old challenges. By creating an environment that encourages experimentation and creativity, regulators aim to position their jurisdictions as hubs for technological innovation and economic growth.

Regulatory Clarity

One of the critical factors in balancing innovation and regulation is the establishment of clear and transparent regulatory frameworks. Ambiguity in regulations can stifle innovation as businesses grapple with uncertainty about compliance and legal requirements. Governments are increasingly realizing the importance of providing regulatory clarity to guide businesses and investors in the cryptocurrency space. By defining clear rules and guidelines, regulators seek to create an environment where innovation can thrive within defined boundaries.

Consumer Protection

As innovation accelerates, ensuring the protection of consumers becomes paramount. Cryptocurrencies and blockchain technologies, while revolutionary, can expose consumers to risks such as fraud, hacking, and market manipulation. Regulatory measures, including stringent know your customer (KYC) and anti-money laundering (AML) requirements, are implemented to safeguard consumers, and maintain the integrity of financial systems. Striking the right balance between consumer protection and the promotion of innovation requires a nuanced and adaptive regulatory approach.

Industry Collaboration

Balancing innovation and regulation involve collaboration between regulators and industry stakeholders. Governments recognize the importance of engaging with the private sector, startups, and industry experts to gain insights into emerging technologies, trends, and potential risks. By fostering open lines of communication, regulators can adapt their approaches based on industry feedback, ensuring that regulations remain relevant and supportive of ongoing innovation.

Sandboxes and Pilots

Regulatory sandboxes and pilot programs provide controlled environments for businesses to test innovative solutions under regulatory supervision. These initiatives allow regulators to observe the practical implications of new technologies, assess potential risks, and tailor regulations accordingly. Sandboxes serve as a middle ground where experimentation is encouraged, providing a valuable bridge between regulatory oversight and the need for innovation.

Gradual Iteration of Regulations

Given the rapid pace of technological change, regulators are increasingly adopting an iterative approach to rulemaking. Rather than implementing static regulations, governments recognize the need to evolve alongside the industry. By regularly reviewing and updating regulations, regulators can adapt to emerging challenges and opportunities, ensuring that the regulatory framework remains responsive to the dynamic nature of the cryptocurrency and blockchain space.

International Collaboration

The global nature of cryptocurrency and blockchain technologies necessitates international collaboration in regulatory efforts.

Governments recognize that harmonizing regulatory approaches on an international scale is essential to prevent regulatory arbitrage and create a consistent framework for businesses operating across borders. Forums such as the Financial Stability Board (FSB) and the Financial Action Task Force (FATF) facilitate collaboration and the development of common standards.

Innovation Hubs

Some jurisdictions are establishing innovation hubs to attract and nurture innovative companies in the cryptocurrency space. These hubs provide a supportive environment, offering guidance on regulatory compliance, access to resources, and opportunities for collaboration. By creating spaces where innovation is encouraged and supported, governments aim to position themselves as leaders in the global digital economy.

Ethical Considerations

As technology evolves, ethical considerations become increasingly important in the regulatory landscape. Governments are tasked with addressing not only the legal implications of emerging technologies but also the ethical challenges they present. Balancing innovation with ethical considerations involves navigating issues such as privacy, data security, and the responsible use of advanced technologies like artificial intelligence within the cryptocurrency space.

Public Awareness and Education

Governments recognize the importance of raising public awareness and providing education about cryptocurrency and blockchain technologies. Understanding the intricacies of these technologies is crucial for both consumers and businesses. Regulatory efforts include public awareness campaigns and educational initiatives to ensure that individuals are well-informed about the risks and benefits associated with participating in the cryptocurrency ecosystem.

XI. Investing in the Future of Cryptocurrency

Risk Management Strategies

Risk management in the context of cryptocurrency and blockchain technologies is a multifaceted challenge that requires a comprehensive and adaptive approach. As the industry continues to evolve, businesses, investors, and regulatory bodies must navigate a landscape marked by volatility, technological complexity, and regulatory uncertainty. Effective risk management strategies are essential to mitigate potential threats and capitalize on opportunities in this dynamic environment.

Effective risk management strategies in the cryptocurrency and blockchain space require a proactive and adaptive approach. From due diligence and diversification to cybersecurity measures and contingency planning, stakeholders must navigate a complex landscape marked by innovation and uncertainty. By embracing comprehensive risk management practices, businesses and investors can position themselves to thrive in the dynamic and transformative realm of cryptocurrencies while mitigating potential challenges.

Comprehensive Due Diligence

Thorough due diligence is a cornerstone of effective risk management in the cryptocurrency space. Businesses and investors must conduct comprehensive research on projects, tokens, and platforms before engaging in transactions or investments. This includes assessing the credibility of development teams, scrutinizing project whitepapers, and understanding the underlying technology. Regulatory compliance and adherence to industry standards are also crucial considerations in the due diligence process.

Diversification of Portfolios

Diversification is a fundamental risk management strategy that applies across various investment domains, including cryptocurrencies. Spreading investments across different assets helps mitigate the impact of a poor-performing asset on the overall portfolio. Diversification extends beyond cryptocurrencies to include different types of assets, industries, and geographic regions, providing a more balanced and resilient investment approach.

Risk Assessment Frameworks

Establishing and adhering to risk assessment frameworks is essential for businesses and investors navigating the cryptocurrency landscape. These frameworks should include mechanisms for evaluating and quantifying risks associated with market volatility, technological vulnerabilities, regulatory changes, and operational challenges. A systematic approach to risk assessment enables proactive decision-making and risk mitigation strategies.

Continuous Monitoring and Analysis

Given the dynamic nature of the cryptocurrency market, continuous monitoring and analysis are critical components of effective risk management. Regularly tracking market trends, regulatory developments, and technological advancements allows stakeholders to adapt swiftly to changing conditions. Automated monitoring tools and real-time data analysis contribute to timely risk identification and response.

Adoption of Risk Management Technologies

Innovative technologies, such as artificial intelligence and machine learning, play a crucial role in risk management within the cryptocurrency space. These technologies can analyze vast amounts of data, identify patterns, and provide predictive insights into market movements. Automated trading algorithms, equipped with risk management protocols, assist in executing trades based on predetermined risk parameters.

Robust Cybersecurity Measures

Cybersecurity is a paramount concern in the cryptocurrency sector, given the prevalence of hacking incidents and security breaches. Implementing robust cybersecurity measures, including secure wallet solutions, encryption protocols, and multi-factor authentication, is imperative for safeguarding assets. Regular security audits and penetration testing help identify vulnerabilities and ensure that protective measures are up to date.

Regulatory Compliance

Navigating the regulatory landscape is a significant aspect of risk management in the cryptocurrency space. Businesses and investors must stay informed about evolving regulations and ensure compliance with relevant legal frameworks. This includes adhering to anti-money laundering (AML) and know your customer (KYC) requirements, as well as understanding tax implications associated with cryptocurrency transactions.

Contingency Planning

Contingency planning involves preparing for unexpected events and having strategies in place to mitigate their impact. This includes scenarios such as market crashes, regulatory crackdowns, or technological failures. Establishing contingency plans allows stakeholders to respond swiftly to adverse conditions, potentially minimizing losses and maintaining operational resilience.

Education and Training

Investing in education and training programs for employees, investors, and users is a proactive risk management strategy. Enhancing the understanding of cryptocurrency risks, market dynamics, and security best practices contributes to informed decision-making. Education initiatives also foster a culture of risk awareness and responsible engagement within the cryptocurrency ecosystem.

Insurance Coverage

As the cryptocurrency industry matures, the availability of insurance coverage tailored to digital assets is increasing. Obtaining insurance against specific risks, such as hacking or theft, can provide an additional layer of protection. However, it's crucial to carefully review policy terms, conditions, and coverage limits to ensure alignment with the unique risks associated with cryptocurrencies.

Identifying Promising Projects and Technologies

Identifying promising projects and technologies in the ever-evolving landscape of cryptocurrency and blockchain requires a combination of strategic analysis, due diligence, and a keen understanding of industry trends. As the sector continues to mature, investors, businesses, and enthusiasts seek opportunities that demonstrate innovation, sustainability, and long-term potential. As the industry continues to evolve, staying informed, conducting thorough research, and assessing projects based on their technological innovation, real-world applications, and community engagement are essential for making informed investment and partnership decisions. Here are key considerations for identifying projects and technologies with promising prospects:

Thorough Research and Due Diligence

A fundamental step in identifying promising projects is conducting thorough research and due diligence. This includes a comprehensive examination of the project's whitepaper, team members, development roadmap, and the underlying technology. Scrutinizing the credibility and experience of the project's founders and developers provides insights into the team's ability to execute the proposed vision.

Technological Innovation and Uniqueness

Promising projects often stand out through technological innovation and uniqueness. Projects that introduce novel solutions to existing challenges or pioneer advancements in blockchain technology are likely to attract attention. Evaluating the technical aspects of a project, such as its consensus algorithm, scalability, and security features, helps gauge its potential for long-term success.

Real-World Use Cases

Projects with real-world use cases and practical applications tend to have greater potential for adoption. Identifying projects that address tangible problems or enhance existing processes in industries such as finance, supply chain, healthcare, and governance adds credibility to their value proposition. Practical utility and relevance contribute to the sustainability of a project.

Community Engagement and Support

The level of community engagement and support can be indicative of a project's potential success. Actively involved and supportive communities demonstrate enthusiasm and confidence in the project. Forums, social media channels, and community-driven initiatives can provide valuable insights into the sentiments of stakeholders and the overall health of a project.

Partnerships and Collaborations

Strategic partnerships and collaborations with reputable entities enhance the credibility and potential of a project. Partnering with established businesses, industry leaders, or academic institutions not only validates the project's legitimacy but also opens doors to valuable resources, expertise, and market access.

Development Roadmap and Milestones

A well-defined and realistic development roadmap with achievable milestones is a positive indicator of a project's viability. Assessing the progress made by a project against its roadmap helps investors and stakeholders gauge the team's ability to deliver on promises and meet set objectives. Transparency and accountability in achieving milestones contribute to building trust.

Regulatory Compliance

Projects that prioritize regulatory compliance and transparency are likely to attract more institutional and mainstream interest. Regulatory adherence fosters a sense of legitimacy and reduces uncertainties related to legal challenges. Projects that proactively address compliance issues and work collaboratively with regulators demonstrate a commitment to long-term sustainability.

Tokenomics and Economic Model

Examining the tokenomics and economic model of a project is crucial for understanding its long-term viability. Factors such as the token distribution, utility within the ecosystem, and mechanisms for incentivizing stakeholders contribute to a project's economic sustainability. A well-designed tokenomics model aligns the interests of participants and supports the project's growth.

Track Record and Reputation

A project's track record and reputation within the industry are valuable indicators of its potential. Projects with a history of successful development, adherence to timelines, and positive community interactions are more likely to gain the trust of stakeholders. A strong reputation establishes credibility and positions a project for sustained success.

Market Trends and Adaptability

Keeping an eye on market trends and a project's adaptability to changing conditions is crucial. The cryptocurrency and blockchain space is dynamic, and projects that demonstrate the ability to evolve in response to market demands and technological advancements are more likely to thrive over the long term. Adaptability and agility are key qualities of promising projects.

Long-term Investment Perspectives

Long-term investment perspectives in the cryptocurrency and blockchain space involve a strategic approach that goes beyond short-term market fluctuations. As the industry matures, investors are increasingly recognizing the potential for sustained growth and value creation. Adopting a long-term investment perspective in the cryptocurrency and blockchain space requires a strategic and forward-looking approach. Investors who prioritize fundamental analysis, real-world impact, technological innovation, and effective risk management are better positioned to navigate the complexities of the industry.

By staying informed, diversifying portfolios, and recognizing the evolving nature of the market, long-term investors can position themselves to capture sustained value and growth in the dynamic world of cryptocurrencies. Here are key considerations for adopting a long-term investment perspective in the dynamic world of cryptocurrencies:

Fundamental Analysis

Long-term investors in the cryptocurrency space often prioritize fundamental analysis over short-term price movements. This involves evaluating the intrinsic value and potential of a project based on factors such as its technology, use case, development team, partnerships, and overall market demand. A deep understanding of these fundamentals helps investors identify projects with strong growth potential over an extended time horizon.

Adoption and Real-World Impact

Projects that demonstrate real-world impact and widespread adoption are attractive to long-term investors. Identifying cryptocurrencies and blockchain projects that address tangible problems and contribute to mainstream adoption is a key consideration. Solutions with practical applications in industries such as finance, healthcare, supply chain, and governance are more likely to stand the test of time and provide long-term value.

Technological Innovation

Technological innovation is a crucial factor for long-term success in the cryptocurrency space. Long-term investors look for projects that not only leverage existing technology effectively but also contribute to advancing the industry. Innovations in consensus algorithms, scalability, security, and interoperability are indicative of a project's ability to remain relevant and competitive over the years.

Market Trends and Evolution

Keeping an eye on market trends and the evolution of the cryptocurrency ecosystem is essential for long-term investors. Recognizing shifts in technology, regulatory developments, and market dynamics allows investors to adapt their strategies accordingly. The ability to foresee industry trends and position investments to capitalize on emerging opportunities is a hallmark of successful long-term investment perspectives.

Diversification and Risk Management

Long-term investors understand the importance of diversification and risk management. Rather than concentrating investments in a single asset, diversification across different cryptocurrencies, blockchain projects, and even traditional asset classes helps mitigate risk. Long-term success is often built on a well-balanced and diversified portfolio that can weather market volatility and unforeseen challenges.

Regulatory Awareness

Regulatory considerations play a significant role in the long-term viability of cryptocurrency investments. Long-term investors stay informed about regulatory developments globally and assess how regulatory frameworks may impact their investments. Projects that proactively address compliance issues and work collaboratively with regulators are often viewed favorably by long-term investors who prioritize stability and legal certainty.

Strong Governance and Leadership

The strength of governance structures and leadership within a project is a critical factor for long-term investors. Transparent decision-making processes, community involvement, and effective leadership contribute to the overall sustainability of a project. Investors look for projects with strong governance models that can navigate challenges and make informed decisions for the benefit of the ecosystem.

Network Effects and Community Support

Long-term success in the cryptocurrency space is often associated with network effects and community support. Projects that attract a growing user base and foster an engaged community are more likely to thrive over time. A vibrant and supportive community contributes to the resilience of a project, providing valuable feedback, fostering innovation, and driving adoption.

Economic Models and Tokenomics

Investors with a long-term perspective carefully evaluate the economic models and tokenomics of projects. Sustainable economic models ensure that a project's native tokens have utility and are designed to align the interests of various stakeholders. Long-term investors look for projects with tokenomics that promote ecosystem growth, incentivize participation, and create a sustainable economic framework.

Evolution of Use Cases

The ability of a project to adapt and expand its use cases over time is a consideration for long-term investors. Projects that can evolve and address changing market demands demonstrate versatility and resilience. Long-term perspectives involve an understanding of how a project's use cases may evolve and whether it can remain relevant in an ever-changing technological landscape.

XII. Conclusion

Summarizing Key Insights

In summary, navigating the diverse and dynamic landscape of cryptocurrency and blockchain technologies requires a holistic understanding of key insights spanning various dimensions. From the foundational definition and brief history of cryptocurrency to the exploration of innovative technologies like blockchain and smart contracts, the journey unfolds with a profound examination of the industry's evolution.

The early stages of cryptocurrency witnessed the rise of pioneers like Bitcoin and Litecoin, setting the stage for the broader altcoin ecosystem and the advent of tokenization. As the sector matured, regulatory developments and challenges came to the forefront, emphasizing the need for a delicate balance between fostering innovation and ensuring consumer protection. The evolution toward Blockchain 3.0 and beyond introduces novel concepts such as interoperability solutions, quantum resistance, and the integration of artificial intelligence, shaping the future trajectory of the industry.

Decentralized finance (DeFi) emerges as a transformative force, marked by concepts like decentralized exchanges, smart contracts, and decentralized lending and borrowing. Alongside opportunities, DeFi brings forth challenges that demand a nuanced understanding of the sector's potential and risks. The tokenization of real-world assets, including real estate and art, represents a significant shift, while security tokens and regulatory compliance mechanisms underscore the need for a regulated yet innovative ecosystem.

The rise of non-fungible tokens (NFTs) introduces a paradigm shift in digital ownership, impacting various industries and redefining how we perceive and trade digital assets. Exploring future trends in tokenization sheds light on the continuous evolution of the industry, emphasizing themes like central bank digital currencies (CBDCs), motivations for their adoption, and their potential impact on traditional banking systems.

Cryptocurrency's role as a store of value, the challenges and solutions for mass adoption, and the implications for cross-border transactions and financial inclusion paint a comprehensive picture of its significance in the everyday economy. Addressing security concerns, the role of privacy coins, and the legal and ethical implications underscore the importance of responsible innovation in the quest for broader societal acceptance.

Beyond financial considerations, the exploration extends to the environmental concerns associated with cryptocurrency, prompting a discussion on sustainable practices and solutions. Cryptocurrency's potential for social change, philanthropy, and community development reveals its broader impact beyond financial transactions. The examination of national and international regulatory frameworks illuminates the complex interplay between global cooperation and local regulatory nuances.

The cryptocurrency and blockchain narrative are a multifaceted tapestry that intertwines technological innovation, economic considerations, regulatory landscapes, and societal implications. The journey from defining and understanding the basics to delving into advanced concepts underscores the transformative nature of this industry. As stakeholders navigate through challenges and opportunities, the overarching theme remains one of continuous evolution, adaptation, and the pursuit of a future where decentralized technologies play a central role in shaping the way we transact, communicate, and perceive value.

Speculations on the Future of Cryptocurrency

The future of cryptocurrency is a realm filled with speculations, intriguing possibilities, and the potential for transformative change across various sectors. As technological advancements continue to redefine the landscape, the speculative outlook encompasses a range of exciting developments that could shape the trajectory of the cryptocurrency space.

One prominent speculation revolves around the concept of decentralized finance (DeFi) gaining further prominence. DeFi has already disrupted traditional financial services by providing decentralized alternatives to banking, lending, and trading. The future could witness an even more extensive integration of DeFi into mainstream financial systems, potentially redefining how individuals' access and manage their finances. This evolution may lead to increased financial inclusivity, efficiency, and a shift toward decentralized systems of governance.

Another compelling speculation centers on the continued growth and evolution of non-fungible tokens (NFTs). The rise of NFTs has already transformed the art and entertainment industries, introducing new possibilities for digital ownership and monetization. Looking ahead, NFTs could extend their influence into diverse domains, including gaming, virtual reality, and even real-world asset representation. The intersection of NFTs with augmented reality and virtual reality technologies may create immersive digital experiences that redefine the concept of ownership in the digital realm.

The advent of central bank digital currencies (CBDCs) represents a significant area of speculation regarding the future of money. Several countries are exploring or piloting CBDCs as a digitized form of national currency issued by central banks. The successful implementation of CBDCs could potentially streamline financial transactions, enhance monetary policy tools, and address issues like financial inclusion. However, challenges related to privacy, security, and interoperability need to be addressed for CBDCs to become widely adopted on a global scale.

The speculation surrounding the integration of artificial intelligence (AI) in cryptocurrency systems adds an intriguing layer to the future outlook. AI has the potential to enhance security measures, optimize trading strategies, and automate various processes within the cryptocurrency ecosystem. Smart contracts and decentralized applications (DApps) could benefit from AI-driven innovations, leading to more sophisticated and adaptive systems.

Quantum resistance is another frontier of speculation within the cryptocurrency community. As quantum computing technologies advance, the cryptographic algorithms currently used in blockchain systems could face vulnerabilities. Speculations involve the development of quantum-resistant algorithms to safeguard the security of cryptocurrencies in a quantum computing era. Achieving quantum resistance is seen as a crucial step in ensuring the long-term viability and security of blockchain networks.

Interoperability solutions represent a speculative avenue that could shape the future of blockchain networks. Overcoming the challenges of siloed blockchains and enabling seamless communication between different blockchain protocols may lead to a more interconnected and versatile ecosystem. The realization of interoperability could facilitate cross-chain transactions, data sharing, and the development of a unified blockchain infrastructure.

Environmental concerns associated with cryptocurrency mining have sparked speculations around the adoption of sustainable practices. As the industry acknowledges the ecological impact of energy-intensive proof-of-work consensus mechanisms, there is a growing interest in transitioning toward more energy-efficient consensus models, such as proof-of-stake. Speculations involve the development of eco-friendly blockchain networks that prioritize sustainability without compromising security and decentralization.

This future speculation on cryptocurrency also extends to its role in geopolitical dynamics. Cryptocurrencies, particularly those designed to be resistant to censorship and control, may play a role in shaping the financial sovereignty of individuals and nations. The ability to conduct borderless transactions and maintain financial autonomy could lead to shifts in global economic power dynamics.

The speculations paint a vivid picture of a dynamic and evolving landscape in cryptocurrency. From the integration of decentralized finance and the continued rise of NFTs to the exploration of quantum resistance, interoperability, and the potential impacts of AI, the cryptocurrency space is a fertile ground for innovation and transformation. As the industry navigates through uncertainties, one thing remains certain: the future of cryptocurrency holds the promise of reshaping how we interact with value, ownership, and the very foundations of the financial system.

Encouraging Responsible Innovation and Adoption

Encouraging responsible innovation and adoption within the cryptocurrency and blockchain space is paramount to fostering a sustainable and inclusive ecosystem. As the industry continues to evolve, stakeholders, including developers, regulators, businesses, and users, play crucial roles in shaping its trajectory. Responsible innovation involves balancing technological advancements with ethical considerations, regulatory compliance, and a commitment to mitigating potential risks.

One key aspect of responsible innovation is the promotion of transparency and open communication. Projects and businesses operating in the cryptocurrency space should prioritize clear and transparent communication about their objectives, technology, and governance structures. Providing stakeholders with accurate and accessible information helps build trust, reduces uncertainty, and contributes to a more informed decision-making process.

Regulatory compliance is a cornerstone of responsible innovation. Developers and businesses within the cryptocurrency space must proactively engage with regulatory frameworks, staying abreast of evolving laws and guidelines. Collaborative efforts between industry participants and regulators can foster a regulatory environment that supports innovation while ensuring consumer protection, financial stability, and compliance with legal requirements.

Responsible innovation extends to addressing environmental concerns associated with certain consensus mechanisms, notably proof-of-work. Encouraging the adoption of more energy-efficient consensus models, such as proof-of-stake, contributes to sustainability and aligns with broader efforts to reduce the carbon footprint of blockchain networks. Projects that prioritize environmentally friendly practices demonstrate a commitment to responsible innovation.

Inclusivity is a key principle in encouraging responsible adoption. Efforts should be made to ensure that the benefits of cryptocurrency and blockchain technologies are accessible to a diverse range of users, irrespective of geographical location or socio-economic status. This inclusivity can be achieved through educational initiatives, user-friendly interfaces, and the development of solutions that cater to the needs of a global and diverse user base.

Education and awareness campaigns are instrumental in promoting responsible adoption. Users, investors, and the broader public should have access to accurate and unbiased information about the risks and benefits of engaging with cryptocurrencies. By fostering a better understanding of the technology, its applications, and potential risks, stakeholders can make informed decisions and contribute to a more responsible adoption of blockchain solutions.

Security considerations are paramount in responsible innovation. Projects should prioritize robust cybersecurity measures, conduct regular security audits, and implement best practices to safeguard users' assets and data. Responsible adoption involves creating a secure environment where users can confidently participate in blockchain activities without undue concerns about hacking, fraud, or other security breaches.

Responsible innovation also involves anticipating and addressing ethical implications associated with emerging technologies. As artificial intelligence and other advanced technologies become integrated into blockchain systems, ethical considerations such as data privacy, algorithmic fairness, and the responsible use of technology must be at the forefront of development efforts. Ethical guidelines and frameworks can help guide developers and businesses in making responsible choices throughout the innovation process.

Community engagement is a critical component of responsible adoption. Projects should actively seek feedback from their user communities, address concerns, and involve stakeholders in decision-making processes. Engaging the community in a transparent and inclusive manner fosters a sense of ownership and responsibility among users, leading to a more resilient and sustainable ecosystem.

Encouraging responsible innovation and adoption in the cryptocurrency and blockchain space requires a multifaceted approach that considers technological advancements, regulatory compliance, ethical considerations, and inclusivity. By promoting transparency, adhering to regulatory standards, prioritizing sustainability, fostering inclusivity, and addressing security and ethical concerns, stakeholders can collectively contribute to building a resilient and responsible ecosystem. As the industry continues to mature, the emphasis on responsible practices becomes increasingly crucial for ensuring the long-term success and positive societal impact of blockchain technologies.

XIII. Glossary

Key Terms of Cryptocurrency

Cryptocurrency:

Definition: A digital or virtual form of currency that uses cryptography for security and operates on a decentralized ledger called a blockchain.

Blockchain:

Definition: A distributed, decentralized ledger that records transactions across a network of computers, providing transparency and immutability.

Bitcoin:

Definition: The first and most well-known cryptocurrency, created in 2009 by an anonymous person or group known as Satoshi Nakamoto.

Altcoin:

Definition: Any cryptocurrency other than Bitcoin. Examples include Ethereum, Ripple, and Litecoin.

Wallet:

Definition: A digital tool that allows users to store, send, and receive cryptocurrencies. Wallets can be hardware-based or software-based.

Mining:

Definition: The process by which new cryptocurrency coins are created and transactions are added to the blockchain. It involves solving complex mathematical problems.

Decentralization:

Definition: The distribution of control and decision-making across a network rather than relying on a single central authority.

Smart Contract:

Definition: Self-executing contracts with the terms directly written into code. They automatically execute and enforce the terms of an agreement when predefined conditions are met.

ICO (Initial Coin Offering):

Definition: A fundraising method where a new cryptocurrency project sells its tokens to early investors in exchange for funding.

Token:

Definition: A unit of value issued by a project through an ICO. Tokens can represent various assets, rights, or access within a specific blockchain ecosystem.

Fork:

Definition: A split or divergence in the blockchain, resulting in two separate chains with different transaction histories. Forks can be soft (compatible) or hard (incompatible).

Exchange:

Definition: Platforms where users can buy, sell, and trade cryptocurrencies. Examples include Coinbase, Binance, and Kraken.

Private Key:

Definition: A cryptographic key that allows access to a user's cryptocurrency funds. It must be kept confidential and secure.

Public Key:

Definition: A cryptographic key that is shared openly and used to generate a unique address for receiving cryptocurrencies.

Hash:

Definition: A fixed-size numerical value computed from input data using a cryptographic hash function. Hashes are used for data integrity and security.

DApp (Decentralized Application):

Definition: An application that runs on a decentralized network, often utilizing smart contracts. DApps aim to be more resistant to censorship and fraud.

Consensus Mechanism:

Definition: The process by which nodes in a decentralized network agree on the state of the blockchain. Common mechanisms include Proof of Work (PoW) and Proof of Stake (PoS).

Cold Wallet:

Definition: A cryptocurrency wallet that is not connected to the internet, providing enhanced security against online threats.

Market Cap:

Definition: The total value of a cryptocurrency in circulation, calculated by multiplying the current market price by the total circulating supply.

Hashrate:

Definition: The speed at which a mining machine or network is able to solve complex mathematical problems. It is a measure of the computational power in a blockchain network.

Concepts of Cryptocurrency

Cryptographic Security:

Concept: The use of cryptographic techniques to secure transactions and control the creation of new units. Cryptography ensures the integrity and confidentiality of data in the cryptocurrency ecosystem.

Decentralization:

Concept: The distribution of control and decision-making across a network of participants, eliminating the need for a central authority. Decentralization enhances security and reduces the risk of a single point of failure.

Blockchain Technology:

Concept: A distributed ledger that records all transactions across a network of computers. Each block contains a cryptographic hash of the previous block, creating a secure and immutable chain.

Mining:

Concept: The process by which new cryptocurrency coins are created, and transactions are added to the blockchain. Miners use computational power to solve complex mathematical problems.

Consensus Mechanisms:

Concept: Protocols used to achieve agreement on the state of the blockchain. Examples include Proof of Work (PoW), Proof of Stake (PoS), and Delegated Proof of Stake (DPoS).

Wallets:

Concept: Digital tools that store private and public keys, enabling users to send and receive cryptocurrencies. Wallets can be software-based (online, desktop, mobile) or hardware-based (physical devices).

Smart Contracts:

Concept: Self-executing contracts with the terms directly written into code. Smart contracts automatically execute and enforce predefined conditions without the need for intermediaries.

Tokenization:

Concept: The process of representing real-world assets or rights as digital tokens on a blockchain. Tokens can represent ownership of assets, access to services, or participation in a project.

Initial Coin Offering (ICO):

Concept: A fundraising method where a new cryptocurrency project sells its tokens to investors in exchange for funding. ICOs provide early backers with tokens that may appreciate in value.

Forks:

Concept: Events where a blockchain splits into two separate chains with different transaction histories. Forks can be soft (compatible) or hard (incompatible).

Altcoins:

Concept: Any cryptocurrency other than Bitcoin. Altcoins may serve different purposes or use alternative technologies compared to the original cryptocurrency.

Decentralized Finance (DeFi):

Concept: A movement that aims to recreate traditional financial systems (lending, borrowing, trading) using decentralized technologies such as blockchain and smart contracts.

Central Bank Digital Currency (CBDC):

Concept: Digital currencies issued by central banks. CBDCs aim to provide a digital representation of a country's official currency.

Non-Fungible Tokens (NFTs):

Concept: Unique digital assets that represent ownership or proof of authenticity for specific items, often used in digital art, collectibles, and gaming.

Privacy Coins:

Concept: Cryptocurrencies designed to enhance user privacy by implementing features that obscure transaction details, such as Monero and Zcash.

Cross-Border Transactions:

Concept: The ability of cryptocurrencies to facilitate transactions across national borders without the need for traditional banking intermediaries.

Regulatory Compliance:

Concept: Adherence to legal and regulatory requirements governing the use and exchange of cryptocurrencies. Compliance measures vary globally.

Security Tokens:

Concept: Tokens that represent ownership of real-world assets, such as stocks or real estate. Security tokens are subject to securities regulations.

Quantum Resistance:

Concept: The development of cryptographic algorithms and protocols that are resistant to attacks by quantum computers, which could potentially threaten current encryption methods.

Environmental Impact:

Concept: The consideration of the ecological footprint of cryptocurrency mining and blockchain operations, with a focus on sustainability and energy efficiency.

XIV. Resources and References

Books:

1. **"Mastering Bitcoin" by Andreas M. Antonopoulos**
   - A comprehensive guide to Bitcoin and cryptocurrency technologies, suitable for both beginners and advanced users.
2. **"The Age of Cryptocurrency" by Paul Vigna and Michael J. Casey**
   - Explores the history and impact of cryptocurrency on the financial world, providing insights into the technology's potential.
3. **"Blockchain Basics: A Non-Technical Introduction in 25 Steps" by Daniel Drescher**
   - An accessible introduction to blockchain technology and its applications, with a focus on real-world examples.
4. **"Digital Gold: Bitcoin and the Inside Story of the Misfits and Millionaires Trying to Reinvent Money" by Nathaniel Popper**
   - Chronicles the history of Bitcoin and the pioneers who played a significant role in its development.
5. **"The Internet of Money" by Andreas M. Antonopoulos**
   - A collection of talks by Antonopoulos, offering insights into the philosophical and economic aspects of cryptocurrency.
6. **"Blockchain Revolution" by Don Tapscott and Alex Tapscott**
   - Explores the transformative potential of blockchain technology across various industries.
7. **"Cryptoassets: The Innovative Investor's Guide to Bitcoin**

and Beyond" by Chris Burniske and Jack Tatar**
    - Provides a framework for understanding different types of cryptoassets and their investment potential.
8. **"The Basics of Bitcoins and Blockchains" by Antony Lewis**
    - A beginner-friendly guide to Bitcoin and blockchain technology, covering essential concepts.

Articles:

1. **"Bitcoin: A Peer-to-Peer Electronic Cash System" by Satoshi Nakamoto**
   - The original whitepaper that introduced Bitcoin and the concept of blockchain.
2. **"Ethereum Whitepaper" by Vitalik Buterin**
   - The foundational document that outlines the design and capabilities of the Ethereum blockchain.
3. **"The Promise of Blockchain" by Marco Iansiti and Karim R. Lakhani (Harvard Business Review)**
   - Examines the potential impact of blockchain technology on business and industries.
4. **"A Letter to Jamie Dimon" by Andreas M. Antonopoulos**
   - A response to Jamie Dimon's criticism of Bitcoin, providing a counterargument in support of cryptocurrency.
5. **"The Flippening: Ethereum vs. Bitcoin" by Chris Burniske**
   - Explores the potential for Ethereum to surpass Bitcoin in market capitalization and influence.

Websites:

1. Bitcoin.org[1]
    - The official website for Bitcoin, providing resources for beginners and developers.
2. Ethereum.org[2]
    - The official website for Ethereum, offering documentation and updates on the Ethereum blockchain.
3. CoinDesk[3]
    - A leading cryptocurrency news platform, providing articles, market analysis, and in-depth features.
4. CoinMarketCap[4]
    - A comprehensive cryptocurrency market data platform, offering real-time prices, charts, and market capitalization.
5. CryptoCompare[5]
    - A platform that provides cryptocurrency data, charts, and analysis for both beginners and experienced traders.
6. The Block[6]
    - A news and research platform focused on the cryptocurrency and blockchain industry.
7. Cointelegraph[7]
    - A popular cryptocurrency news outlet covering a

---

1. https://bitcoin.org/

2. https://ethereum.org/

3. https://www.coindesk.com/

4. https://coinmarketcap.com/

5. https://www.cryptocompare.com/

6. https://www.theblockcrypto.com/

7. https://cointelegraph.com/

wide range of topics and developments in the crypto space.

Reading these resources will provide you with a solid understanding of the history, technology, and current developments in the world of cryptocurrency. Keep in mind that the cryptocurrency space is dynamic, so staying informed through reputable sources is crucial.

Interviews with Industry Experts

1. **Andreas M. Antonopoulos:**
   - **Interview:** "The Internet of Money" on London Real
   - **Key Topics:** Bitcoin, decentralized technologies, and the future of money.
2. **Vitalik Buterin:**
   - **Interview:** "Ethereum's Founder on the Future of Crypto" on TechCrunch
   - **Key Topics:** Ethereum, smart contracts, and the broader blockchain ecosystem.
3. **Catherine Wood (ARK Invest):**
   - **Interview:** "The Future of Finance" on Real Vision Finance
   - **Key Topics:** Cryptocurrency as an investment, blockchain disruption, and financial innovation.
4. **Balaji S. Srinivasan:**
   - **Interview:** "The Future of Bitcoin" on Tim Ferriss Show
   - **Key Topics:** Bitcoin, decentralized technologies, and the potential impact on society.
5. **Laura Shin:**
   - **Interview:** "Unchained" Podcast
   - **Key Topics:** Various interviews with industry experts covering a wide range of cryptocurrency and blockchain topics.
6. **Roger Ver:**
   - **Interview:** "The Bitcoin Gospel" on London Real
   - **Key Topics:** Bitcoin, Bitcoin Cash, and the philosophy of cryptocurrency.

7. **Ari Paul (BlockTower Capital):**
   - **Interview:** "Invest Like the Best" Podcast
   - **Key Topics:** Cryptocurrency investments, market trends, and the evolving landscape.

8. **Raul Pal:**
   - **Interview:** "The Future of Money" on Real Vision Finance
   - **Key Topics:** Macro perspectives on Bitcoin, cryptocurrency as a store of value.

9. **Dan Morehead (Pantera Capital):**
   - **Interview:** "Blockchain & Cryptocurrencies" on Bloomberg
   - **Key Topics:** Cryptocurrency investments, market analysis, and blockchain's impact on finance.

10. **Meltem Demirors:**
    - **Interview:** "Unchained" Podcast
    - **Key Topics:** Bitcoin, blockchain, and the evolving regulatory landscape.

(Please note that the availability of these interviews may change over time, and it's a good idea to search for the most recent content or new interviews with these and other industry experts to stay updated on the latest insights and perspectives in the cryptocurrency space.)